W9-CNA-948

SCHOOL MAINTENANCE & RENOVATION

School Maintenance & Renovation

Administrator
Policies,
Practices,
& Economics

Dr. Glen I. Earthman and Dr. Linda Lemasters

PRO>ACTIVE PUBLICATIONS

School Maintenance and Renovation

Published by:
Pro>Active Publications
1148 Elizabeth Avenue #2
Lancaster, Pennsylvania 17601 U.S.A.

Printed in the United States of America
10 9 8 7 6 5 4 3 2 1

Entry under main title:
School Maintenance and Renovation

ISBN: 1-885432-26-7

Contents

Preface

COLLECTIVELY, the citizens of the United States have a tremendous investment in community infrastructure, which includes a vast array of expensive structures devoted to local services, such as libraries, court buildings, and schools. The subject of this book is the public school system infrastructure, the buildings and their contents that serve K–12 students and teachers. It has been estimated that the investment the country has in school buildings is in excess of $1 trillion, which represents the replacement cost of the buildings. The investment has been accumulating for over a century and would be impossible to duplicate in current dollars.

This irreplaceable investment must be kept intact and in good working order. Today, most school systems find it difficult just to find the funds to properly maintain the existing stock of buildings, let alone build new structures. This work focuses on the fiscal and personnel costs of school maintenance and renovation. What does it take in terms of financial and human resources to keep school facilities at a high level? What are the routines and the calculations that enable school leaders to do this efficiently?

The importance of proper maintenance of school buildings cannot be overstated. Of even more importance is the realization that the physical environment in which education is conducted has an influence upon the achievement of students. During the past decade, research has offered data demonstrating that the condition of the school building affects student learning, either in a negative or positive manner.

The knowledge that the citizens of the country have a considerable monetary and emotional investment in the buildings used for education, plus the fact that these buildings play an important role in the proper education of children mandate diligence in the care of school buildings. This volume gives the practicing administrator both basic and sophisticated tools for understanding how to prolong the useful life of school buildings. At the same time, the book explains what it costs to operate a school building. In addition, a detailed plan of how school renovations are carried out is presented —with a view to attaining and preserving educational ends. The true costs of maintenance and renovation are analyzed, and important saving mechanisms are provided. With this volume, educators can learn where and where *not* to apply cost-cutting mechanisms in the daily operation of schools and in plant improvement.

Intended Audiences

This book is written for decision-makers in school buildings, district offices, and boards. This includes principals and other administrators, who are legally responsible for keeping buildings safe and orderly. Research findings have demonstrated that principals are very aware of the condition of the building they are administering and perhaps know the condition better than the central administration (Brannon, 2000). In addition, principals usually instigate and inspect school repairs.

The intended audience also includes decision-makers in private and parochial schools. In fact, this publication should be of special help to administrators in this section of education. Many times, the administrators in this sector do not have a staff to conduct the maintenance program for the school system such as their counter parts in the public school systems have. The administrator may have little or no support staff to help keep the buildings in good condition. Therefore, it falls to the administrator to not only keep the educational program functioning at a high level of effectiveness, but also to do those things to keep the building working efficiently. In the private and parochial sector, there are many educational organizations that consist of one school building with one administrator to do all of the tasks in operating the school. There may or may not be a governing board that has expertise in maintenance work, but sometimes the principal or administrator is the sole individual responsible for the "whole show." This person needs practical assistance in discharging the responsibilities of properly maintaining the buildings. This individual, therefore, should this book especially useful.

In all sectors of the educational establishment in the country, there is a need for properly trained individuals who can assume the responsibility of conducting a maintenance program. Replacement personnel in the maintenance program are constantly needed, and this book provides important background to train such individuals.

Sources of Help

TODAY there are many sources of assistance in helping individuals or staffs in doing their job in maintaining a school building in good condition or in successfully completing a modernization project on an existing school building. The sources listed below include both print and non-print materials that contain excellent material. The print material contains a listing of books and journals. The electronic sources include web sites and electronic journals, and finally there is a listing of professional organizations that provide professional development activities of interest to people in this field of work. Further, the web pages also have links to other sources. In many cases, the material available through these sources is either free or inexpensive.

Print Sources

Books

Castaldi, B. (1994). *Educational facilities: Planning, modernization, and management.* 4th edition, Boston: Allyn and Bacon, pp. 1–379.

CEFPI. (1993). *Guide for planning educational facilities.* Scottsdale, AZ: The Council. pp. 1–124.

Earthman, G. I. (1994). *School renovation handbook:* Investing in education. Lancaster, PA: Technomic Publishing Company. pp. 1–180.

Earthman, G. I. (2000). Planning educational facilities for the next century. Reston, VA: The Association of School Business Officials, International. pp. 1–299.

Earthman, G. I. (2001). Experiencing a renovation: A practical guide for principals. Reston, VA: National Association of Secondary School Principals. pp. 1–44.

Journals

Educational Facility Planner, Scottsdale, AZ: Council of Educational Facility Planners, International.

National School Boards Journal, Alexandria, VA: National School Boards Association.

School Business Affairs, Reston, VA: The Association of School Business Officials, International.

School Planning & Management, New York: Paul Abramson, editor.

Electronic Sources of Help On-line

Electronic Journals
The Technology Source - http://horizon.unc.edu/TS
K–12 Tech Watch - k12techwatch@lists.eschoolnews.com

Web Sites
National Clearinghouse for Educational Facilities - http://.www.edfacilities.org
School News online - http://www.eschoolnews.org
Price Watch - http://pricewatch.com
M&O Information - http://www.SchoolDude.com
Construction Data - http://www.schoolconstructionnews.com
Technology Source - http://ts.mivu.org
School Facilities News - http://www.schoolfacilities.com
Mississippi State University Educational Design Institute - http://www.sarc.msstate.edu
Randy Fielding Design Studio - http://www.designshare.com
North Carolina School Design Clearinghouse - http://www.schoolclearinghouse.org
Automated Building Systems - http://www.automatedbuildings.com/
http://www.caba.org/aboutus/public_info.html

Professional Organizations

The following organizations provide professional development activities for individuals engaged in maintenance and renovation work on school buildings.

Association of School Business Officials, International
11401 North Shore Drive, Reston, VA 20190
(703) 478-0405
www.asbointl.org

Council of Educational Facility Planners, International
9180 Desert Cove Way, Suite 104, Scottsdale, AZ 85260
(480) 391-0840
www.cefpi.org

National School Boards Association
1680 Duke Street, Alexandria, VA 22314-3493
(703) 683-7590
www.nsba.org

Association of Physical Plant Administrators
1643 Prince Street
Alexandria, Virginia 22314-2818
Phone: 703-684-1446
Fax: 703-549-2772
www.appa.org

National School Plant Management Association
P. O. Box 8010
Lexington, KY 40533-8010
(877) 833-0610
www.nspma.com

Government Agencies

U.S. Department of Justice
950 Pennsylvania Avenue, NW
Civil Rights Division - Disability Rights Section
New York Avenue Building, Room 4023
Washington, DC 20530
http://www.usdoj.gov/crt/ada/adahom1.htm

U.S. Equal Employment Opportunity Commission
1801 L Street, N.W.
Washington, D.C. 20507
http://www.eeoc.gov/teledir.html

CHAPTER 1

How Schools are Funded

THE mechanism and formulas used by the various states to fund local public schools are so complicated and multi-layered that an extensive discussion would necessitate many volumes. In addition, the sources of revenue used by the states to secure funds for schools vary considerably. Likewise, the manner in which private and parochial schools are funded varies from institution to institution.

In this chapter only basic principles are presented about how public, private, and parochial schools in the United States obtain their funds. The intent of this section of the book is to review several critical revenue sources in the overall school finance picture. To those in authority in the private and parochial sector who are not familiar with public school funding, this chapter offers elementary insights into the problems public school authorities face in obtaining resources for their operation. The material is presented as background to further discussions on the financing of school maintenance and renovation.

The Reserve Clause of the United States Constitution places the responsibility for education on the individual states. Therefore, each state offers an educational program to all children and youth within a prescribed age limit. In all cases, the constitution of each state guarantees every student in that jurisdiction a basic educational program. The educational program offered by one state is nominally different from the programs offered by other states, yet there is a great deal of commonality of basic programs across the United States. As a result, the basic educational requirements are virtually the same in every state. There may be a difference in terminology, but the requirements are almost identical.

State Responsibility

Even though the state mandates a basic educational program, the state has

1

placed the responsibility of operating the schools upon the local authority, regardless of what that governmental entity might be. Historically, the organization of the local school system has been on the lowest unit of government. In some cases, this has been on the township basis, reflecting the requirements of the Northwest Ordinance of 1797, according to which the local unit of government was the township, and the township became responsible for operating the school. There are other governmental structures upon which school systems are organized. In many states, special districts are created for the purpose of providing educational services. These districts can span other governmental units or be contained within a single unit, e.g., a county. These districts are considered quasi-governmental units devoted to a single purpose, that of providing educational services. The school district is the most common form of governmental unit that provides educational services in the United States. In some states, the county and/or city is the lowest governmental unit, and the county/city provides educational services in addition to other services. Thus, the local school system is coterminous with the boundary of the county or city.

Because of the diffused responsibility for education, each state has had to devise a uniform system for funding the educational function. These programs have been based upon the traditions and requirements of each state. As a result, there is a great variety of funding programs and each is indigenous to the particular state. Each state determines the extent of the educational program it will fund. Educational programs that exceed what the state requires are the direct financial responsibility of the local school system, and local funds must be generated to fund such programs, including some capital campaigns.

The state provides money to each local school system for the required basic educational program. The state determines what constitutes the basic educational program and funds that portion of the total program offered by the local school. These moneys are derived from the general budget of the state, which is funded by the various streams of tax revenue generated by the state. The streams of tax revenue generally come from the: income tax, sales tax, personal property tax, license fees of various sorts, sale of property, and rental fees. There may be other specialized taxes or assessments employed by states to generate general revenues (i.e., some states have devoted all or a portion of the lottery revenues to education). Funds given to the local school system are generally termed grants, because the money is used by the local school system to provide state-mandated educational programs to students.

Local School Responsibility

Almost every local school system provides educational programs and services to students above what is required by the state. As a result, these program and service extensions must be paid for by local revenues. These funds are usually obtained by using the tax mechanism the state has permitted the local government to use. In almost every case, this has been a tax upon the real estate or property of individuals and businesses located within the confines of the school system. By levying a tax on all real estate located in the school system, revenue is obtained to pay for school programs and services. These taxes are termed *ad valorem* because they are assessed based upon the value assigned to real estate being taxed. *Ad valorem* taxes are the main source of revenue for local governmental units, including school systems. The tax is a very stable source of revenue and does not fluctuate as much from year to year as do other tax bases. On the other hand, the real estate tax is not very responsive to changing economic conditions such as inflation and recession. In addition, this tax is not as efficient as other forms of taxes because of the high administrative costs and limited tax base. The real estate tax is not considered a progressive tax in that it falls the heaviest on large property owners such as farmers and on the older population. Nevertheless, the real estate tax is the basis of funding for both operational and capital fund needs by the local school system. The same observation regarding the diversity of state funding programs that is made for the funding efforts of the educational program can be made for funds that are used to construct and maintain buildings. There are differences in each state, but there is a great deal of commonality in how the local school system obtains funds for capital improvement projects. Historically, states have placed the responsibility of raising capital funds for school buildings on the local school system.

The precise reasoning for this may be lost in history, but it can be assumed that from the time of the colonists the entire cost of providing educational services to students fell to the local community to provide. Not only the costs of a teacher, but also where the teacher would conduct classes, were the responsibility of groups of families or the community itself. The state did not enter into the equation of funding education until well into the eighteenth century. As a result, the place where education takes place was entirely up to the local community. This tradition has held sway down to the present. That notwithstanding, many states now have been called upon to provide funds for the construction of new facilities and even the maintenance of existing school buildings.

Local School Bonds

The most common method local school authorities have of financing capital improvement projects of all sorts is through the use of bond funds. Local school systems in almost every state have the authority to go into debt by issuing municipal government bonds, which are also called General Obligation Bonds. There are some exceptions to this in those states, such as Virginia and North

Carolina, where the local school board is not fiscally independent of the local governmental authority. In these situations, the school board must ask the local government to go into debt to fund capital improvements. The general obligation bonds are a direct debt of the school system, issued to obtain funds for capital projects. The bonds are repaid by levying a special tax upon the real estate owned by citizens of the school system.

School boards and boards of education obtain the authority to issue bonds through passage of a bond referendum. The bond referendum is a simple vote of the electorate to enter into debt to raise funds for capital projects. In most states, a simple majority of the votes is needed for approval to float bonds. There are, however, some states that require a higher vote count. Some states require a 67 or 75 percent approval rate before the bond referendum is approved. In 2002, the State of California reduced the percentage of votes necessary for a bond issue to pass from 66 percent to 55 percent.

There are localities where the school governing body can vote to go into debt without approval of the electorate. These cases are unusual and require certain circumstances to be evident. As an example, cities in Virginia have the constitutional authority to vote to go into debt to the extent of 10 percent of the total assessed valuation without voter approval.

Following voter approval, the school board begins the process of approving and selling the bonds to obtain funds for the various projects under consideration. Bonds are sold on the competitive market through an open-bid procedure. School boards employ bonding expertise to insure the legality of the bonds, to suggest an acceptable interest rate, and to actually sell the bonds. Normally, large investment or bond companies bid upon the bonds in order to market the bonds for the school system. The bonds are sold to various investment firms in exchange for funds that are forwarded to the school system to use for the capital projects. Once the proceeds from the bond sales are received by the school system, they are expended through the normal business processes to contractors and vendors for services rendered and for equipment purchases related to the project. Funds obtained through the sale of municipal bonds are highly restricted, in that they must be used for capital purposes and may not be used for operational purposes. In fact in some jurisdictions, the funds are specifically earmarked for projects and cannot be spent on other projects without permission from voters.

Local School Debt

The debt from the bond sales is entered into the annual budgetary system of the school district. The term of a municipal bond is usually twenty years, and the school system pays off the debt through annual installments through the debt service section of the annual operating budget. Special taxes are imposed upon the inhabitants of the school system to provide for the extra funds needed to retire the bond indebtedness.

There are many issues and problems associated with the management of the indebtedness of a school system. Debt service can be a large drain on resources of the school system if it reaches certain limits. Debt service must be kept within a certain payment range, so as not to heavily impact the operating budget. The old premise that the more funds needed for debt service, the less available for educational programs, has a great deal of authenticity. Additionally, the amount of debt a school system carries on its books can negatively impact its credit rating. In turn, this could effectively increase the rate of interest a school system must pay for new indebtedness.

Funding Maintenance

Maintenance work is normally funded from the operational side of the annual budget of the school system. The operating budget is funded from the annual tax levy on real estate. These taxes go directly into the general fund of the school system and are allocated to the different sections of the operating budget. Of course, there are other sources of funds, such as state and federal funds, which are in the operating budget, but often times these funds are for special purposes and can not be used otherwise. Nevertheless, keeping the buildings repaired and operating must be funded from the maintenance and operations section of the annual budget, approved by the school board or board of education.

There are some exceptions to the general rule that maintenance is funded through operating revenue. In some instances, school systems do not have the resources to complete some special projects that require more revenue than would normally be available in the annual budget. Items such as a new roof, a boiler replacement, or a new water system may cost more than the school system has within its annual means. In such cases, the school authorities may well have to go into debt to secure sufficient funds to complete such a project. In small school systems, this scenario may be played out whenever such large projects need to be done. Normally, except for large projects that require a great deal of revenue, maintenance items are not funded from borrowed revenue. The general rule to follow in deciding whether or not a maintenance item should be funded through borrowed funds is that the project or item should be of such magnitude as to require the school system to go into long-term debt. In other words, painting a building is something that needs to be done every 5–10 years. Bond funds are usually paid back over a twenty-year period. The life of the painting job does not exceed the number of years the school system will require to pay back the funds used. Thus, painting projects should be funded through the regular operating funds. The longevity of the maintenance work to be done should at least meet the length of time to retire the indebtedness. The life of a new roof is usually 20–30 years, which is more than the length of time it will take to repay the debt, and such a project would qualify for being funded through bond funds.

State-Funded Programs

In addition, there are some special state-funded programs designed to help local school systems shoulder their maintenance needs. These funds are usually provided on a cost-sharing or matching basis where the state provides a certain percentage of the needed funds and the locality provides the rest. The state of West Virginia has such a program because of the vast amounts of revenue provided localities through the West Virginia School Building Authority to construct new facilities. The reasoning behind this program is that the state has an interest in the good maintenance of the facilities, given that a large amount of the construction costs have been borne by the state. There are other states that provide an annual per-pupil grant for maintenance purposes. These programs are not large, but they do show the interest a state has in the educational facilities of the locality. The U.S. General Accounting Office (2000) reported that in the 1998–99 school year, 15 states provided little or no funding for local capital improvement projects.

Private and Parochial Schools

Private and parochial schools do not enjoy the benefit of a stable stream of revenue from the community to fund maintenance projects similar to that of the public schools. These schools must rely upon either student tuition, private donations, or grants from the church body to fund their operations. Unless the school is wealthy enough to have a substantial endowment that can provide a dedicated source of funds solely for maintenance items, operational funds must be used to complete maintenance projects. Usually a set aside portion of the annual tuition a student pays to attend a school is allocated for maintenance and upkeep of the building. Only the normal maintenance items can be accomplished by these revenues because they are limited. When the school faces a large cost or replacement item, other sources of resources must be used, or some type of fundraiser must be conducted.

A private or parochial school can seek funds from institutions of the banking industry and retire the debt through tuition payments or other revenues received by a church or sponsoring institution. Most parochial schools, at least on the elementary level, are sponsored by a local church or parish. Although the schools are usually financially independent of the church, there may be revenues dedicated for the upkeep of the school building by the church.

Politicization of the Funding Process

Every state has a somewhat distinct funding process, which is applied and implemented at the local level. Perhaps because of this, all the steps to gain funding are interwoven with politics, which is more than a matter of party differences. Funding involves the politics of personalities, opinions, understanding, and personal agendas. This is not an unexpected phenomenon, nor should it be considered a hindrance, as long as what is best for students is the primary concern, and decisions are made based on correct information and good research.

One of the greatest hindrances to school funding is the concept that maintaining the facilities is not a part of instruction. Too many school boards, school administrators, teachers, parents, and communities see facilities and the personnel who maintain them as an auxiliary part of the educational process. Thus, when it is necessary to cut the budget in some area, often it is the custodial, facilities, or grounds items that are considered first, as it is believed that facilities are not a part of instruction. However, research demonstrates that facilities are linked to instruction, that that the condition of the environment where children learn affects both achievement and behavior. It may affect the classroom teacher, too.

A model developed by Cash (1993) best exemplifies a discussion of this process. The first element that directly or indirectly affects the condition of a building is leadership. This may be the leadership of the locality, the leadership of the school division, or leadership at the building level. A breakdown at any one of these level or a lack of acknowledgment of the importance of the facility will eventually affect the physical structure, maintenance, and operations and ultimately the place where the students learn, as necessary funding is not appropriated.

There is a direct connection, too, in how the funding flows for maintenance,

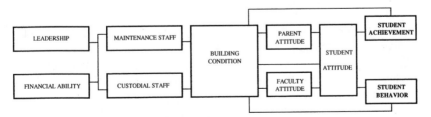

Figure 1-1 Cash's Theoretical Model.

remodeling, and construction. Funding is directly related to the convictions of the leading powers in the state and localities, in addition to the national level, as to the importance of the facility. Often funds are cut for schools as politicians and educators fail to recognize the impact of the facility on the student or the educational process. In Cash's theoretical model, the maintenance and custodial staffs directly relate to the condition of the building. There are two important components that affect the tasks that these employees perform. First, their work is only as good as the funding with which they are provided to accomplish their tasks. Secondly, no matter the level of funding, there must be an explicit mission shared with these staffs that maintenance, custodial tasks, and grounds work are an important part of the total educational process. There must be a shared vision that clean buildings, facilities in good repair, and schools that provide an infrastructure for twenty-first century curricula are important.

The building condition in turn affects the attitudes of three groups of clients: parents, faculty, and students. The effect of buildings on people is a complicated relationship, as the building has a direct influence on the student, as well as an indirect relationship on the student via the parents and faculty. Poor facilities can create numerous negative relationships, e.g., between students and learning or parents and the school. Ultimately, there is a message to all of the stakeholders that education is of lesser importance, when the community fails to fund the appropriate environment for learning (Lemasters, 1997).

While many elements within the educational process are outside of the control of the educator and the community leader, it is possible to provide a school facility that exemplifies to the student the importance that the community, the state, or the nation places on education. This can be accomplished by the community putting the emphasis on the buildings and grounds by providing the funding necessary to keep them neat and operating efficiently and effectively. The place where students learn can encourage good student behavior and optimal student achievement by being safe, clean, and in good repair. As stated by Edwards (1991):

> Good infrastructure is truly at the base of a quality education. For a society searching for ways to address the education needs of the future, the building itself is a good place to start. (p. 47).

Public Law 107–110, the *No Child Left Behind Act of 2001*, addresses many elements of public education in America: student achievement, parental choice, teacher quality, student readiness, and so on. Very little is mentioned about the facility, except for the areas of technology, charter schools, and student safety as it relates to tobacco and crime issues. There was $1.1 billion in the national 2001 budget allocated for school renovation, IDEA-related retrofits, and technology grants. This is in light of a Fast Response Survey System (FRSS) survey indicating that three-quarters of schools in America reported needing to spend some money on repairs, renovations, and modernization, with over $127 billion required to accomplish these tasks (Lewis, Snow, Farris, & Westat, 2000). Therefore, one can conclude that school maintenance is a political issue that needs to be addressed, not only in the state and local arena, but also at the national level. Subsequent chapters will speak to these needs in detail.

References

Alexander, K. and Alexander, M. D. (1992). *American public school law.* St. Paul, MN: West Publishing Company.

Cash, C. S. (1993). *Building condition and student achievement and behavior.* Blacksburg, VA: Unpublished doctoral dissertation, Virginia Polytechnic Institute and State University.

Edwards, M. M. (1991, May). *Building condition, parental involvement, and student achievement in the D.C. public school system.* Unpublished master's thesis, Georgetown University, Washington, DC.

Kozol, J. (1991). *Savage Inequalities.* New York: Harper-Collins.

Lemasters, L. K. (1997). *A synthesis of studies pertaining to facilities, student achievement, and student behavior.* Unpublished doctoral dissertation, Virginia Polytechnic Institute and State University, Blacksburg.

Lewis, L., Snow, K., Farris, E., & Westat. (2000, June). *Condition of America's public school facilities:* 1999 (FRSS Publication No. NCES 2000-032). Washington, DC: U.S. Department of Education, Office of Educational Research and Improvement.

No Child Left Behind Act of 2001, (Public Law 107–110).

United States Constitution, Section 10, Clause 10.

United State General Accounting Office. (1996). *School facilities: Schools are not ready for the next century.* Washington, DC: GAO/HEHS.

CHAPTER 2

Organization of Maintenance, Engineering, and Operations Staff

What Does the Maintenance, Engineering, and Operations Department Do?

IN schools, the department of maintenance, engineering, and operations, which may go by many different departmental names, is dedicated to building maintenance, engineering services, construction, and grounds care. These services are combined to provide a healthy, safe, and pleasant work environment that is conducive to student learning and employee satisfaction. Generally, the department's first responsibility is maintenance and operation of the schools, administrative buildings, and any special support facilities. It also is responsible for grounds maintenance, custodial services, facilities planning, and some construction and remodeling projects.

A facilities maintenance department must be staffed by employees who have a wealth of knowledge about today's sophisticated buildings, operating systems, and myriads of complex environmental and legal challenges. These may include but are not limited to the following tasks:

(1) Planning (long-term and short-range)

(2) Budgeting special projects and developing operating budgets

(3) Maintaining current facilities, including custodial services, engineering services, and operations management

(4) Maintaining grounds and supervising real estate transactions

(5) Overseeing projects, installations, contracted work, construction, and renovations

(6) Coordinating design work and specifications for projects

(7) Assuring that proper coordination occurs between instructional personnel and the facilities department

(8) Making recommendations and developing safety procedures for operations, as well as the work environment.

With such a large range of responsibilities, no longer can the facilities operation be a department of generalist craftspersons. The director must have a vast array of knowledge of various systems, with a staff of specialists in engineering, various crafts, purchasing, legal issues, and expertise in other areas that will assure a safe, accessible, and secure learning environment. To be effective and efficient, the personnel must be skilled and provided with staff development that will maintain a department on the cutting edge of operational tasks and procedures.

Organization of Maintenance, Engineering, and Operations—Internally

Departments come in all sizes, with responsibilities that range from drawing water samples for testing, replacing a broken floor tile, or installing electrical outlets for new computers, to replacing electric pumps or providing a lesson on safety to a new principal. Some departments are organized by the various skills needed to perform necessary maintenance on school facilities, with a foreman in each area, such as plumbing, electrical, and general maintenance. Other departments have a supervisor that provides the leadership for the whole department and sends out skilled personnel to a job, or that supervisor initiates a crew of workers to provide the service. In many larger school districts, the organization of the department is complex and unique.

The key to an effectively organized maintenance department is to organize so that communication is optimal, within the department and to the department. A school system can have a maintenance department that has the greatest of skills, tools, and ambitious personnel, but if there are not clear lines of communication, the customers of the services may perceive a quite different scenario.

Organization by School

In larger school organizations, there is a chief executive who leads, directs, and manages the facility operation. That individual may have an assistant. The schools and facilities in the system are divided and assigned to maintenance crews who are responsible for the upkeep of those particular facilities. Each crew's assignment in the district reflects a division of tasks that will: allow enough time for quality service, have facilities assigned that are geographically convenient to one another, and/or match the needs of the plant operations to the skills of the maintenance employees in the crew. Figure 2.1 depicts an example

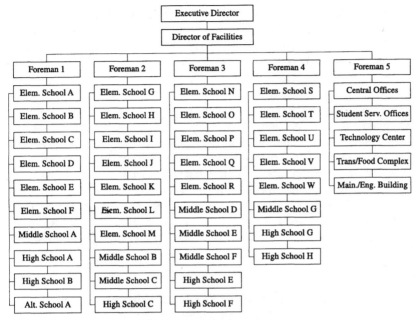

Figure 2-1 Maintenance department in a large school district, organized by school/facilities.

of the organizational chart of a large school district or school organization maintenance department.

These work crews have assistant directors or foremen who pick up the work orders, direct the operation, and coordinate the workday for the greatest efficiency for the schools to which they are assigned. This may include dividing their operations to respond to work orders by skill areas. The foremen should have the ability to work well with principals and other administrators in assuring that not only are the maintenance tasks accomplished, but also in maintaining direct lines of communication with the instructional staff. The goal should be to assure educators that the maintenance department is working to meet the needs of the instructional personnel and to optimize the educational setting.

Organization by Skills

The second way that many maintenance departments are organized is by skill areas. Usually these departments are in mid-size or small systems, which can be efficiently and effectively served by a structure with this type of organization. The division of tasks within the department may be divided differently than is shown in Figure 2.2. Crews within these departments respond *district-wide* to the work orders submitted.

No single template can be used for all school districts. The formula for success is to have a director with planning and organizational skills who can match the skill areas to the needs of the maintenance and engineering tasks to be done. This presupposes a work-order system that is efficient and conducive to meeting the needs of the clientele.

One of the greatest challenges that work crews encounter as they go from job to job is that administrators in the building perceive the presence of the crews as an opportunity to address jobs that were not part of the work order. It is difficult for support personnel to tell administrators that they cannot conduct their tasks in that manner. If they do not stay on task and complete the job on the work order, they will not get to prioritized work in a timely manner. In such cases, the director of the department is responsible for explanations to the administrators why work cannot be conducted in a facility without it being reported on a work order. This communication will enable the department to provide more satisfactory service, to provide service based on a set of previously published priorities, and to maintain estimated timelines for projects and daily schedules.

Placement of Function Within the School System

The placement of the facilities department within the organization is very dependent on the organization of the administration within the school system. Many times the size of the system dictates to whom the Director of Maintenance and Engineering reports. The larger the school district is, the greater likelihood of the manager of this department reporting directly to the superintendent (Figure 2.3). The level of responsibility within the division of the assistant superintendent for facilities is equal to that of the other superintendents in the system (e.g., assistant superintendent for instructional services or human resources).

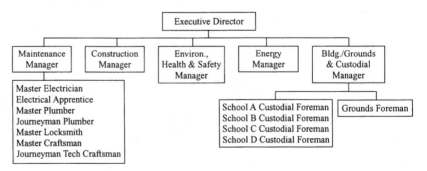

Figure 2-2 Maintenance department in a mid-size/small school district, orgainizes by skill area.

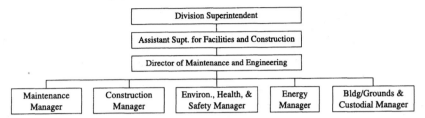

Figure 2-3 Placement Within the School District.

In smaller systems, the facilities director may report to the assistant superintendent for administration services or the executive director of finance. Whatever the placement of the function is within the school district, there should be an organizational concept that portrays the importance of the function to the school district or organization. The engineering department should be placed on the organizational chart in such a way that its director and other employees have access to higher management.

Lines of Responsibility and Authority

The importance of the functions and tasks of the facilities department merits a position within the organizational chart that provides the department with the authority to accomplish the many duties related to the health, safety, and welfare of the school district. The lines of responsibility are also reciprocal. Instructional personnel need to understand the importance of good school maintenance for education. On the other hand, maintenance personnel need to feel a part of the instructional team. This relationship is often fragile and overlooked

There are over 90,000 school facilities in the United States, with three-fourths of them having been built more than thirty years ago. This statistic alone exemplifies the enormity of the mission of the maintenance employees. Without the appropriate authority to accomplish this vast responsibility, the chances of successfully meeting the challenge are greatly reduced. Without maintenance personnel understanding their importance and impact on the classroom, the instructional mission will be impaired.

Relationship with Other Departments in the School System

Communication
The key to effective and mutually beneficial working relationships is effec-

tive communication. School facilities management is no exception. If the facilities manager aspires to any level of success, he or she must understand this fully and strive to maintain clear lines of communication with the total school operation. In order to accomplish this task, a quick review of certain communication skills is necessary.

(1) *Make sure the sender and receiver of the message understand that both parties are interested in the message.* The lines of communication should be so clear and a level of trust so evident that both the sender and receiver are assured that the message being sent is important. Too often, the instructional administrator perceives that the facilities department takes complaints and work orders too lightly. A well-managed organization will engender few complaints or perceptions that the facilities department is not responsive.

(2) *Assure that the sender and receiver believe that all parties are knowledgeable about the message.* The instructional personnel need to be confident that the facilities workers understand the importance of meeting the needs of the instructional program. Along the same thought process, the facilities department, to operate efficiently and effectively, requires a level of understanding from the instructional department that there may be higher priorities, schedules to keep for other projects, or simply a backlog of work.

(3) *Strive to recognize the frequent bias of the sender or the receiver.* Often when the maintenance department receives a work order about a temperature problem, roof leak, or any one of a myriad of daily reports, it is one request of dozens; or it may be a complaint that has been repeated daily. It is easy for the facilities manager to be jaundiced by this repeated barrage of requests. Once this bias occurs, the respondent may begin to perceive that his or her needs are not being met. The facilities manager must work to make sure that the message is not perceived as being avoided or misinterpreted (Snowden & Gorton, 2002).

The school board and district superintendent are responsible for communication policies that define the expectations for communication between departments, as well as the channels of communication for personnel. The administration is charged with putting in place regulations and practices that facilitate these lines of communication and enhance such opportunities rather than impede. These practices need to include written guidelines for communication (letters, memoranda, e-mail, and work orders), as well as clear lines for a chain of command to report needs and seek assistance.

Organizational Placement

School districts locate the maintenance, operations, and engineering department in their organization in nearly as many different ways as there are school systems. As noted in Figure 2.3, some departments report directly to the district superintendent. In other, usually smaller, departments, the facilities operation may be a part of administrative services, a part of the business and finance department, or some other configuration that meets the needs of the school district and matches the expertise of the personnel. No matter what the placement in the school organization, it is important for the school board and district superintendent to include the operations personnel in the leadership processes. Maintenance personnel need to understand their roles in the instructional mission.

When new programs are planned, a representative from the facilities department should be a part of the planning to answer questions and review maintenance schedules, plant layouts, and laws or regulations that may inhibit certain usages. If there is an instructional council that meets regularly, maintenance and engineering should be a part of that organization.

Size and Expertise of the Department

Occasionally in administrative meetings in school districts, one hears statements implying that the maintenance and operations department is not a part of the instructional program. This may impact decisions, especially during budget time, with governing bodies cutting the budget of the facilities departments. Shortsighted leadership may suggest that decisions were made to shortchange the budget of operations and maintenance because budgetary allotments are devoted to instruction only. However, if operations and maintenance are not funded, instructors will not have the support necessary to maintain a safe, healthy, and comfortable learning environment. Most teachers will quickly share with members of a maintenance crew the negative impact on their instructional day when the room temperature was out of control or there was a steady stream of water dripping from a leak.

How does a governing body know what the funding should be to provide the correct number of maintenance workers, with the necessary expertise? A school district must develop a standard for the condition of its schools and equipment and hire the personnel and purchase or keep in good repair the equipment necessary to maintain that standard. The director of the department ought to determine employee work levels and monitor them consistently. Job descriptions, work assignments, and equity in distributing tasks are essential to maintenance supervision.

Personnel management in a maintenance department requires full utilization of staff, along with prudent control of overtime. Management must allot time for maintenance of equipment, purchasing and organizing of supplies, traveling between assignments, and taking necessary breaks. According to the *California State Department of Education's Administration of Maintenance and Operations in California School Districts,* approximately 40 percent of the normal workday may be spent in such activities. Effective foremen will work to make the time on the job more efficient and to minimize the off-task time.

Maintenance departments can no longer hire only general maintenance employees. Technology advances, building codes and regulations, and the complexity of today's facilities require maintenance and operations employees who are specialists. Employees must understand and be able to repair: bell and clock systems, video surveillance, sophisticated heating, ventilation, and air conditioning systems (HVAC), lighting and HVAC energy saving systems, and more. No single formula exists to determine the specialists that a school organization will need to adequately meet the personnel needs of the maintenance and operations departments. The maintenance director and other school administrators should assess the district needs and develop a roster of specialists.

Sometimes a particular skill is demanded within a district; however, the workload does not merit a full-time employee in that area. Hiring someone to do the job part-time is not an option because most electricians, plumbers, and other master technicians want full-time employment. Therefore, the only option is to contract out the work. This can be accomplished by having a company or person on retainer, which can sometimes be less expensive, as the contract can be negotiated; or, the jobs can be let as they become available.

The department director, working with the human resources department, should make sure that an accurate job description is written for each position within the facilities department. The job description will include information about the qualification requirements for the position, the person to whom the position reports, information about the evaluation process, and examples of the tasks to be performed. If there are physical requirements for the position, they should be clearly and explicitly delineated, as there are legal implications as per the Americans with Disabilities Act, if such requirements are not clearly stipulated.

Attempting to project the number of custodians necessary for facilities may be more quantitative than maintenance projections. The California Association of School Business Officials has generated several guidelines.

	Formula
Teacher Factor	1 Custodian Per 8 Teachers
Pupil Factor	1 Custodian Per 225 Students
Room Factor	1 Custodian Per 11 Rooms to be Cleaned
Square Footage Factor	1 Custodian Per 15,000 Square Feet of Facility

Figure 2-4 Area Allotment Per Custodial Employee.

Denver, Colorado Public Schools developed a formula based on the following important elements:

(1) School site
(2) Building units such as classrooms, offices, health services, library
(3) Kindergartens
(4) Lunchrooms and multipurpose rooms
(5) Auditoriums
(6) Heating plant
(7) Plumbing fixtures
(8) Gymnasiums
(9) Community use of buildings
(10) Square footage of building.

These elements are judged in conjunction with the number of minutes necessary to complete various tasks.

No matter what the formula used to assess the number of custodial personnel needed for a school district, it is up to the maintenance director to ascertain whether or not the personnel are being used efficiently, are keeping the facilities clean and pleasant, and are working well with the other employees in the facility. Custodians should have an aptitude for problem solving, be willing to meet the unique needs of the building staff, and be able to stay on task, even with many interruptions and distractions.

Maintenance Personnel Costs

According to a recent report in the AS&U magazine, support is "dwindling" for school expenditures for maintenance and operations of facilities (Agron, p. 24). Such a funding trend does not bode well for salaries or workload. The square footage maintained per custodian increasing from 21,156 to 22,222 indicates that more work is being demanded from fewer employees, often without commensurate compensation.

Agron reported that modest salary increases were reported for the following three maintenance positions:

- Median salaries for maintenance personnel were $29,213 (up 5 percent from the previous year;
- Median salaries for grounds personnel were $23,858 (up 3 percent); and,
- Median salaries for custodians were $22,686 (up less than one percent from the previous year.

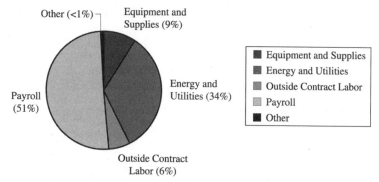

Figure 2-5 Average Division of Maintenance and Operation Costs.

A market study would need to be conducted by a locality or school organization to assess the appropriate salary guidelines for each area of the nation.

By what areas is the maintenance budget allocated? According to a national survey, the maintenance and operations budget is divided in the following manner:

This division of funds within the maintenance department does not reflect what is generally held for personnel costs in the total school organization. Most school divisions spend approximately 70 to 80 percent of their budgets on salaries and benefits. Therefore, it appears that not only are dollars allocated for maintenance and operations disappearing, but also the salaries for the personnel are not emphasized as much as those in other departments of the school operation.

Principal's Responsibility in Maintaining Schools

The principal of a school building has a responsibility to maintain the school building, but in most public school organizational structures has little direct line authority over the staff charged with that responsibility. As distressing as that may seem, it does not mean that the principal is helpless. Quite the contrary, a principal has a great deal to do with the condition of a school. Considerable research has been completed in the last decade identifying the influence a building in good condition has on the performance of students (Lemasters, 1997). These studies have identified a relationship between the condition of school buildings and student scores on achievement tests. In some studies (Berner, 1993; Cash, 1993; Earthman et al, 1995; Hines, 1996), the difference in achievement scores between students in poor buildings and students in functional buildings has been as high as 11 to 14 percentile rank points. This difference in student achievement scores illustrates the fact that students perform much better in schools that are in good condition than they would if they were in poor buildings.

Well-run schools presuppose a good working relationship between the maintenance personnel and the school principal. The principal is always concerned with the physical environment in which the students learn, especially as it relates to safety and hazards. The school leader must constantly be on guard to eliminate any conditions that can cause harm to students, either in themselves or because of negligence on the part of school personnel. The principal is responsible for the safety of all students, faculty, staff, and visitors to the building. As such, the principal must know what constitutes a safety hazard and be aware of possible safety hazards in and around the school building and grounds. This perception is acquired through courses on legal aspects of education taken in the principal preparation program at universities and through on-the-job experience. The legal responsibility of the principal regarding the safety and well being of everyone in the school is extensive. Because of this, a principal must do everything within the power of that office to make certain the building is in good condition.

A school principal is normally in direct line authority to the superintendent of schools, which means the principal is a line officer with all of the authority conferred by the school board to administer an educational program housed in a safe school building. The principal is the immediate supervisor of all teachers, support staff, and clerical assistants. The principal also has complete control over the use of the building during the time the students and teachers are in attendance. Often, the superintendent holds the principal responsible for the condition and appearance of the school building.

In the usual line and staff organizational chart of the school system, a principal does not have any immediate line authority over maintenance and operations staff or generally the cafeteria staff. The principal usually does not have authority to either employ or discharge any of these employees because their immediate supervisor is someone in the central administration of the school system. The principal may have some evaluative input for these employees, but that input must go through appropriate channels to the superintendent and then from the superintendent to the appropriate office or director for maintenance/operations or food services. In small school systems, the line of communications may be directly from the principal to the director of maintenance and operations, even though there is no line of authority there. Such communications reflect an informal internal organization of the school system. Regardless of the size of school system, this approach to communication and evaluation of employees can lead to problems. Under these circumstances, considerable good will and cooperation are required for smooth working relations between the principal and the custodian, maintenance, and food service staffs.

The question arises as to how a principal can have much control over the condition of the school building if the employees in the school answer to someone in the central administration. The principal does have a direct line to the superintendent and can use that position to bring about changes to improve the condition of the school building. This is almost like a "bully pulpit" for the principal to make changes.

A principal should establish a goal to have a clean and well functioning building at all times. The level of cleanliness desired by the principal needs to be determined in conversations with the custodian, so that the latter can understand expectations required. The principal must inspect the appearance of the school every day and work with the custodians to achieve that level of cleanliness. An effective principal does not tolerate a dirty building.

Building inspections by the school principal

In addition to normal order and safety, school principals have a double responsibility for building maintenance. In the first place, the principal should identify and report immediately any conditions that need the attention of the maintenance department. Some of these conditions are emergencies, such as a broken window or a malfunctioning heating system. The principal is the first line for getting something done to correct the condition and is also the person legally charged with such requests. The principal should inspect the school building and grounds daily for conditions that need attention or correction. These conditions must be reported immediately through set channels of communication. Most school systems have an emergency request process whereby maintenance personnel can be brought to bear on a condition that must be corrected immediately. A principal must be aware of such systems and not be reluctant to use them. Teachers and staff must also be aware of such reporting processes and inform the principal of any conditions that need immediate attention.

The second aspect of the responsibility of the principal in maintenance applications is to identify conditions that need to be changed or repaired to make the school more functional and efficient. These items are not emergencies and usually must be prioritized for funding. Identification of these conditions is usually done through an annual inspection tour of the building. The items identified through this tour are major. The principal, custodian, and others e.g., teachers, should be involved in the tour. The outcome of the tour is to make prioritized recommendations to the director of maintenance and operations for items to be included in the maintenance budget for the next fiscal year.

The annual inspection tour is normally done to coincide with the preliminary preparation of the school system's operating budget. The maintenance items and work are identified as a result of the tour, and these are then forwarded to the director of maintenance and operations to be included with the needs of other schools to form the department's budget request.

References

Agron, J. (2002, April). *Dwindling Support.* AS&U. Retrieved on August 25, 2002, from www.asumag.com.

Berner, M. M. (1993, April). Building conditions, parental involvement, and student achievement in the District of Columbia Public School System. *Urban Education,* 28(1), pp. 6–29.

Cash, C. S. (1993). *Building condition and student achievement and behavior.* Unpublished doctoral dissertation, Virginia Polytechnic Institute and State University, Blacksburg.

Earthman, G. I., Cash, C. S., and Van Berkum, D. (1995, September). A statewide study of student achievement and behavior and school building condition. Paper presented at the annual meeting of the Council of Educational Facility Planners, International, Dallas, TX.

Hines, E. W. (1996). *Building condition and student achievement and behavior.* Unpublished doctoral dissertation, Virginia Polytechnic Institute and State University.

Lemasters, L. K. (1997). *A synthesis of studies pertaining to facilities, student achievement, and student behavior.* Blacksburg, V A: Unpublished doctoral dissertation, Virginia Polytechnic Institute & State University.

Snowden, P. E. and Gorton, R. A. (2002). *School leadership and administration: Important concepts, case studies, & simulations.* McGraw-Hill Higher Education: New York, NY.

Note: For information on personnel costs, please see the following Internet site retrieved on August 25, 2002: *http://www.business.com/directory/human_resources/compensation_and_benefits/salary/index.asp?partner=primedia*

CHAPTER 3

School Board Policies for Maintenance and Operations

O NE way to assure that appropriate planning for school facility and operations maintenance occurs is to have needed policies in place for environmental, buildings, grounds, and property management. Effective management of facilities can take place only when there is appropriate planning. Part of that planning process is to develop policies, which will include timelines, problems personnel should report, scheduling for maintenance needs, guidelines for purchasing, decision-making, and collaboration. It is the responsibility of the school board to set the policies. The administration then develops regulations to enforce the board's policies.

Often, policy development is reactive. Something occurs, a question arises, and a policy is developed to take care of the situation the next time it happens. This is not the ideal way to develop policies and procedures. It is much better to be proactive, rather than reactive. It is not necessary when accomplishing this to try to discover on one's own what, where, and when a policy is needed. Look to state professional organizations, state departments of education, and other school divisions when developing policies. These recommendations are appropriate for public and private schools.

How Policies Are Developed

The National School Board Association (NSBA) has suggested several noteworthy steps in policy development. Many school organizations throughout the nation follow these steps and provide the guidance necessary to make decision making within the schools and districts easier.

(1) The issue of the problem should be defined. When a policy is in place, the

school board and the administration will find it easier to decide what the decision should be and who should make it. The policy needs may be generated by national and state laws, safety issues, local pressures, or any one of innumerable problems or challenges.

(2) After the issue is defined about which there is a policy need, the superintendent and administration should work to discover all related issues and information. To do this, they should seek sample policies from national organizations, state departments of education, and other school districts. The staff member in charge of developing the draft policy may want to speak with colleagues in other districts, seek the advice of community members, and always keep the district superintendent in the information loop.

(3) Since policy is the school board's domain, the draft should be discussed with the board members. At this point in development, NSBA recommends that several questions be raised:

    (a) Is the policy consistent with national, state, and local laws?

    (b) Does it meet with the school district's mission and goals?

    (c) Is it good practice and reasonable?

    (d) Does it cover the subject and is it limited to one policy topic?

    (e) Is it consistent with existing policies?

    (f) Can it be administered as a practical, affordable policy? This last question about cost is of great importance for the purposes of this text. Every policy has a cost, and these costs must be analyzed in light of the safety of staff and students, amortization over the life of an operation, and local funding mechanisms. An unfunded mandate is often a non-mandate.

(4) The draft is now ready to be written in its final form for the first reading. This reading should be shared with the school board, of course, along with the district superintendent and affected stakeholders. Policy put into force without this step will result in problems of intelligibility and interpretation.

(5) After input from the first reading, appropriate revisions should be made and the second reading held.

(6) At this time, the policy is ready for adoption and distribution to the public and stakeholders.

(7) The last step, often omitted, is the evaluation process. A well-written policy often has a stipulation and timeline for evaluation. This assists in keeping the policy from becoming obsolete, as well as modifying the policy if certain aspects do not meet the needs and expectations of the teachers, staff, administration, school board, and the community. One option that always should be considered is to put a time limit on the policy, i.e., a point where it needs to be taken off the books. Too often, policy manuals are packed with outmoded regulations.

Energy Conservation

Building/Grounds Access & Security

Disaster Plans

Safety & Fire Drills

Emergency Plans

Vandalism & Grafitti Removal

Purchasing & Outside Contracts

POSSIBLE Policy Topics

Evaluation of Systems

Evaluation of Personnel

Accident Reports

Replacement Cycles & Insurance Management

Buildings & Grounds Maintenance

Playground Maintenance & Inspections

Laws, Codes, & Regulations

Figure 3-1 Possible Policy Topics.

What Kinds of Policies Are Needed for an Efficient Department?

No single policy guideline informs a district how to run an efficient plant and operation. Several general areas should be considered for policy management (Figure 3.1).

The policies for maintenance, buildings, and grounds should support an efficient maintenance operation, provide for the safety of students, employees, and the community, and provide an umbrella under which staff can direct an effective and efficient operation. The school board should set policies that direct the mission of the support services departments, without hampering the operations with too much detail. It takes a collaborative effort of the administration and board to fine tune this balance.

Legal Consultation

Many school boards require that the school attorney review all policies prior to board approval. The legal review should occur near the beginning of policy development. The legal consultant can be very useful in noting appropriate legal references, as well as helping the school board and administration to keep from omitting components or including items that could get the school organization into legal difficulties.

Development of Regulations

Once policies are in place, the superintendent or the school administration is charged to develop any necessary regulations to implement the policy. For instance, the board may have a policy in response to state code about fire drills. A regulation would be published by the administration to provide guidelines on procedures to conduct such drills.

Reference

National School Board Association. *Policy development steps.* Retrieved May 30, 2002, from http://www.nsba.org/sbot/toolkit/PolSteps.html.

CHAPTER 4

Administrative Process—The Paper Chase

How Can Costs Associated with Maintenance Procurement Be Controlled?

MANY school districts have an office in the finance department or in the local government that is in charge of procurement. Its guidelines and regulations may be set by the state government, the locality, or the local school district-or all three. No matter what these guidelines are, most organizations have long recognized procurement as a key way to make sure that the best is purchased for the least investment. It is important to recognize that procurement is not just getting the lowest price, but it is also making the procurement decision at the right time, keeping a lean inventory, and considering the long term.

The Procurement Process

Many finance directors and principals are quick to share their woes concerning the jumble of rules, regulations, processes, and procedures for procurement. The paperwork is enough to bring terror to the heart of the most hardened bureaucrat. Spending public funds is serious business, and most purchasing manuals are prime examples of how difficult and cumbersome that process is.

A step in the direction of keeping the cost controlled is a thorough understanding of a school district's buying procedures. How many steps does the process entail? Three? Eight? Fourteen? At what point is a procedure redundant and not providing any additional safety features or efficiency? Administrators must recognize that methods designed to save money in purchasing can actually lose money through wasteful expenditure of personnel time.

Automation

Many procurement processes are automated or are being considered for automation. Such processes can be web-based programs, programs that permit e-purchasing, or simply putting the paperwork on templates for computer access. No matter what the system, if it is designed correctly, there should be a savings in personnel costs, less paperwork, printing, and other copied material. One word of caution, however, the selection of the software for an automated process is of paramount importance. The software should meet the needs of the school system, be affordable to purchase and maintain, and have the support of the supplying company.

Procurement Cards

Many school districts provide schools and departments with procurement cards. These are similar to gift cards in that they have an approved dollar amount. In addition, there are stipulations as to what can be purchased with them. For instance, a maintenance employee in the plumbing department may have a procurement card that is approved for up to $1,000 purchases for plumbing supplies. With this card, the plumber can make purchases of smaller items used on a regular basis. It is estimated that procurement cards can save a purchasing department up to 80 percent of paperwork, time, and personnel costs. Staff then has time to work on larger expenditures, e.g., bids and proposals.

Consolidation

Smaller and mid-size school districts and school organizations have created consortiums for purchasing or are consolidating purchasing with other localities. This permits the school systems and local governments to save funds by making larger purchases and having greater negotiating power. It, also, can be a huge time-saver, with one purchasing staff meeting the purchasing needs of more than one school district, local government, or school. Such consolidation also may be important for private schools. A consortium of privately operated schools may find it beneficial to combine purchases for materials and supplies, cafeteria food, and certain services to achieve an economy of scale.

Consultants

There are many times when purchases need to be made in a school district, and the procurement personnel may or may not have the expertise to make informed decisions as to bidding processes, specifications, and materials that will be the most cost effective. An example of such a purchase may be a roof replacement for a school or a replacement heating, ventilation, and air condition system. Time can be saved and a more efficient process may be gained by using a specialist in the field. Consultants may be used to save money for the purchaser, to assure that a correct system is purchased, to make purchases that last long-term, and to purchase what will be maintainable by the school district.

Consultants can provide information on specifications, vendors, or any one of innumerable pros and cons on specific products.

How Maintenance Projects Are Identified

There are many ways to identify maintenance projects. One such way is to have schedules within the maintenance department that will identify routine projects and assist with regularly servicing systems and equipment. Centralized maintenance personnel must cultivate and work with observant building administrators and custodians. They often can be the "eyes and ears" of the maintenance staff. The following are some of the additional ways that maintenance workers and other school personnel identify projects:

(1) When maintenance employees respond to work orders, often other areas of concern and problems that need attention are noticed and should be reported to the director of projects.
(2) Personnel should develop a checklist of items that are reviewed periodically for the grounds and the facilities. Such review assists in assuring safety and helps to identify problems early. The following are sample groundskeeping areas on such a list:
   - Pedestrian areas, such as sidewalks, steps, and ramps
   - Lawn improvements (give safety features priority)
   - Vehicle traffic areas, such as parking lots (include appropriate lighting with this item), bus loading and unloading zones, ingress and egress to the sites, and many more
   - Playground areas.
(3) There should be a similar list of the interior of school plants and facilities:
   - Plumbing fixtures, such as toilets, drinking fountains, related pipes, and sewer systems
   - Any structural items such as wall, support mechanisms, HVAC systems and equipment, ductwork, and fans
   - Lights and items that may affect appropriate light control, such as wiring, shades, and so on
   - Cosmetic updating: painting, floor coverings, etc.
   - Special school systems and equipment (gymnasiums, clock systems, and lockers).
(4) The third checklist addresses program equipment found in the schools:
   - Technical equipment in the shops, such as automotive, metals, and electronics
   - Furniture for students and teachers in the classrooms, as well as in

special areas such as the library, offices, cafeteria, and so on. The latter item of cafeteria furniture is important because of the safety measures. One of the areas of the highest number of workers' compensation claims comes from improper operation of cafeteria tables

- The office equipment in the business lab
- Any audiovisual equipment
- Science related equipment, furniture, and systems, such as a quick wash for chemical accidents
- Cafeteria equipment, such as refrigeration units, stoves, and fans for ventilation.

(5) The school system should have a planned, cyclical maintenance program for the certain facilities in the organization. Some of the systems that can be on a cyclical program are roofing systems, floor coverings, interior and exterior painting, lighting improvement, furniture replacement, parking lot maintenance, lawn improvements, window and door replacement, lockers maintenance and auditorium seats. This list is just the beginning; however, if there is a cycle for major servicing, maintenance, and replacement, the budget impact can be kept to a minimum and planning is facilitated.

(6) Building personnel are a source of invaluable information about a facility. They are served daily by the system and equipment of a facility and know where the problems are.

Annual Inspections

One way to assure decreased maintenance costs is by expending funds for personnel to conduct annual inspections. Just because a system appears to be working well is not time to forget about it. Periodic inspections and maintenance save time and headaches by identifying potential problems early. Annual inspections, or more frequently if need be, are one way to keep a healthy operation and to uncover potential problems.

Another important reason for a systematic inspection process and a good record-keeping system is to have the ability to share system, equipment, and operation histories with governing bodies. The school board, city council, or county board of supervisors may be more likely to appropriate funding for new equipment and systems, when it is made evident that the old equipment was maintained well and continually monitored.

Hand-in-hand with the inspections should be a good system of record keeping. Equipment histories will help track the quality of a product, or may begin to give subtle hints that trouble is brewing, e.g., a pump slowly losing pressure.

Who is responsible for and included in inspections? First, there should be an organized schedule of inspections. One way to save money on the costs of inspections, as well as the record keeping, is to automate the process. Even small school districts should consider using some type of computer program to assist in scheduling inspections and tracking the data from inspections.

The director of maintenance is responsible for establishing the inspection schedule, the types of information collected, and who will be responsible for the collection of the data. In most instances, the maintenance personnel will be assigned these functions; however, it is important to mention that building personnel should be brought into the process, too. If administrators understand some of the functions and specifications under which the equipment operates, they can let maintenance and operations know if potential problems exist.

The Occasional Maintenance Project

"The best laid plan. . ." may not keep every emergency at bay. It seems that when the budget is tight and the time inconvenient is usually when the "occasional maintenance" situation arises. With planning, these situations can be covered by replacement back-ups or contingency funds. For instance, if a sewer system is totally dependent on a pump that has gone out in the past, perhaps the old pump should be rebuilt and stored. Or, if snow removal equipment for the school district is inadequate for large snowfalls, perhaps the director of maintenance should have a contingency contract with a local firm with snow removal equipment.

There are occasional maintenance projects that are not emergencies but become urgent and require special funding. For instance, the fire marshal or OSHA inspector makes a surprise visit and finds a situation that needs to be corrected. A ramp may need to be installed, a ventilation system may need to be updated, or any one of expected improvements due to a change in the code or regulations. If the funding cannot be found in the regular operating budget, the maintenance director may need to go before the school board to attain a special appropriation, as repairs or renovations required by a regulatory body must be done.

Forms That Are Used in the Requesting Process (See Appendices)

There are a couple of organizational determiners for the types of forms used to submit requests for maintenance work. If a school division has a computerized or web-based system, the computer software may drive the type of form that is used. The organization of the department, as reviewed in an earlier chapter, may influence the informational structure of the form. The administrators and the maintenance personnel may have preferences for submitting the information that will influence the format the forms take.

Capital Projects Work Orders

Many school organizations have different forms (Figure 4.1) for capital improvement projects (CIP) than those used for jobs that are regular service work orders. CIP budget items often have their own line in the organizational budget, usually beginning at around $5,000, and typically represent scheduled renovation, rehabilitation, improvement, or addition. Some school districts not only provide a minimum dollar amount for CIP items, but also note that the project must not be consumable or disposable. The work is scheduled after it is budgeted, and the record keeping is done by project. Often there is a project director or clerk of the works, and the project spans a multi-year time period.

Since the CIP project may be a very large expenditure, it is essential to plan the CIP budget at least five to seven years into the future. Indeed, it may be a ten- to fifteen-year budget document. This assists the local school organization, as well as any governing body, in being able to plan and finance the large projects. The operation becomes even more efficient when projects of this nature can be

DEPARTMENT		PROJECT TITLE			PROJECT MANAGER		
PROJECT DESCRIPTION							
PROJECT JUSTIFICATION							
SOURCE OF FUNDS Local (L) Nonlocal (N)	ESTIMATED TOTAL	RECOMMENDED FUTURE FUNDING					COST BEYOND
SOURCE OF DATA	COST	FY'03	FY'04	FY'05	FY'06	FY'07	FY
COST ELEMENTS	AMOUNT	FY	RECOMMENDED FINANCING		METHOD OF EST.		
Preliminary & Design							
Land Acquisition							
Site Preparation							
Construction							
Landscaping							
Equipment & Furniture							
Legal							
Other Cost Elements							
Contingencies %							
TOTAL							

SUBMITTING AUTHORITY: CONTACT PERSON:

ADDRESS:

TELEPHONE:

SIGNATURE   DATE

Figure 4-1 Capital Improvement Project Request Form.

placed on a cycle. A good example is a cycle for roof replacements. From re-cords, the maintenance director knows the life cycle of a roof. Instead of having two or three schools needing major roof repairs or replacement during the same time span, a cycle can be developed, so that only one moves onto the current CIP budget at any one time. Cycles can be created for furniture replacement, replace-ment of floor coverings, HVAC upgrades, and other systems. The cycle system also should be closely related to the organization's preventative maintenance plan.

Normal Maintenance or Repair Work Orders

Normal repair orders are the projects generated (a) by personnel doing gen-eral maintenance inspections, (b) by vandalism or careless operation of equip-ment or care of a facility, (c) by personnel who are requesting minor changes in the facility to support the instructional program or operation of the district, and (d) by school personnel using the facilities when the custodian cannot conduct the repairs. Generating these requests is the responsibility of the principal, facil-ity administrator, or other designated persons as requested by the maintenance department. The forms used are designed to be effective by supplying the what, where, critical issues, and contact person.

There are probably as many different forms as there are school districts across the nation; however, there are some items that will be found on all, if the mainte-nance department is being run efficiently and effectively. Some of the common characteristics of a work order form are:

(1) Who is generating the work order

(2) Where the problem is

(3) Date and time of the related problem

(4) A description of the problem.

What Office Is Responsible for Processing Requests?

Even though there may be more than one office responsible for responding to a work order request, the work orders should all be submitted to one office. This office will be responsible for seeing that the appropriate services are contacted, the scheduling is done expediently, and the appropriate person signs off on the completed job. Work on requests should begin as soon as possible, and the main-tenance department should have a system to track response time to work orders. Being slow to respond ultimately gives the maintenance department a bad repu-tation with the rest of the employees-who may interpret delay as indifference. There should never be more than a five-day response time, unless someone from the department has communicated to the building administrator about what is causing the delay.

Emergencies, obviously, should be responded to immediately. An emergency is a situation that is life-threatening, could result in serious injury, a problem causing interruption to the instructional program, or a situation that may cause serious permanent damage to property.

For reporting any situation, there should be a clear line of responsibility that is made known to all school administrators. This will provide a proper cost control and eliminate paper work. Each work order should have a corresponding finance element. What is the cost of the labor to complete the job? What do the parts cost? There should be a portion of the work order that provides time data. When was the work order submitted? When was it responded to? How long did the repair take? Were safety and health issues addressed in a manner to reflect their importance? All of these issues deal directly or indirectly with cost, and cost data is a precondition of monitoring departmental efficiency.

Work Order Routing

Part of the process and staff development that the maintenance department should use for the work order system is to maintain a routing procedure. Again, this is another area where communication is critical. An ideal procedure is to have as few steps as possible for the employees and administrators to use to submit an order. If the work order system is not yet computerized, the process still should be only one step for the initiator. The on-site person should be able to send a simple facsimile to the maintenance department to report the problem. If the process is web-based, there should be just one template that goes directly to maintenance.

Once the request has gone to the maintenance department, there should be a single job designator. This may be a highly trained administrative assistant, a foreman, or a computerized assignment system based on the information provided on the request form. If the latter is the method used, there still should be one employee who briefly reviews the assignments.

The assignment brings into play, again, the organization of the maintenance department. If the department is organized by skill area, the request is given to the crew representing that certain skill. If the department is organized by serving a particular group of schools, the request migrates to the crew serving those schools in which the requesting school resides. There are often times when the request process is not that easy. There may be work orders that involve more than one skill area. For example, a roof has leaked and has done damage to ceiling tile. The tile needs to be replaced, the roof may need a patch, and a lighting fixture was damaged, too. In such an instance, a foreman or some other position within the chain of command ought to have the authority to assemble whatever specialists are needed to correct the problem.

Although there should be one person who is ultimately in charge of seeing that work orders are handled as quickly as possible, other personnel and work areas are involved. These may be the inventory manager, the office assistant who manages the budget, the calendar manager, the vendor contact, and any other employee needed to get a repair completed effectively.

Who Decides Whether Work Is Done by Outsiders or In House?

An issue that needs to be confronted is whether to call in outside specialists to handle repair work. How is this decided? The criteria are commonsensical. Does the maintenance department have employees with the right skills to get the job done? If not, the repair needs to be done by an outsider. In the same vein, if the maintenance department does not have the equipment necessary to make the repair or if the equipment cannot be rented, the job will need to be conducted by someone outside. Finally, it may be that the equipment can be rented, but no one in the department can efficiently operate the equipment; again, the decision is relatively easy.

Making a decision of this sort is not always so simple. Several years ago, one of the authors was working for a school division with an excellent maintenance and engineering department, which was perceived to be inefficient, slow to respond, and in general very irresponsible. The district's administration conducted a study to see what the difficulty was, since with such a skilled staff, the department should have been successful. The consultants found that the department was skilled, caring, and efficient with its tasks. However, the employees were doing so many small construction projects and minor alterations that they did not have the time to conduct the general maintenance of the school district. When the director began to employ outside contractors for some of the jobs, the reputation and effectiveness of the department improved greatly. Here, a decision to outsource construction improved the efficiency and response time of the in-house staff.   .

Often the conscientious director will be torn between the needs of the school organization and the budget. The director may know that more jobs can be accomplished if done in-house, but on the other hand, does not want to risk overextending the work force.

The decision to outsource should be made based on a set of criteria approved by the superintendent or the governing body of a private school. Once the criteria are in place, the director of the custodial, maintenance, and engineering department should know when to make the decision to have the job done inside or outside. These criteria should be based on the skills involved, the necessary equipment, time elements, cost, efficiency, and effectiveness. Cost certainly should be one of the more important driving forces, but it definitely is not the only one.

Who Completes the Repair or Maintenance Item?

To determine who actually completes the work, the detailer assigning tasks needs to consider the skill level, the equipment, and the employees who have the time to work on the project. For some of the tasks, such as electrical repairs, the skill area dictates which crew will be sent to conduct the repair. There, also, may be a cooperative agreement with the custodians for them to do specific minor repairs in the building, such as changing light bulbs, replacing ceiling tiles, installing pencil sharpeners, and other routine maintenance jobs.

No matter what procedure is used to assign the work, it needs to be a process that is not time consuming. When the crews arrive at work each day, the work order assignments need to be ready to be acted on. Assignments can also be made at the end of the previous day or even two days in advance.

The following is an example of an assignment procedure. A request arrives from a school or other initiation point. In this particular example, the work request is computer generated. The controller assigns the work order by skill areas in two-day increments. This is done to provide for the greatest efficiency in assembling supplies and materials. The worker always knows one day in advance the approximate type of materials that are necessary and where the next job will be. Assignments made over a three-day period may overwhelm the employees with the number of tasks. Before the worker leaves the site, some response must be entered into the work-order template before the next job can be started. That response may be that the job was successfully completed or a part needs to be ordered or any other status information about the job. It provides an accountability element to the process. In this particular school district, there is a computer available to the maintenance worker at each school or facility, and job completion information is entered into the computer CMMS program by the maintenance employee.

In general it is advisable that the work crews work an earlier shift than other school personnel, to avoid interrupting the school day. In fact, there may be some repairs and alterations that cannot be done during the school day. Either they are unsafe or would cause too great of an interruption. Certain schools have large maintenance crews that work only afternoon, evening, or early morning shifts.

The Feedback System

The work-order process needs to contain a procedure that allows for feedback to the maintenance department as well as to the initiator of the request. This may be as simple as having duplicate copies of the work order request form, which both parties keep after the job has been completed. It may be a computerized process that provides a way for the maintenance department to respond to the building administrator as to what was done, the time it took, the cost of materials, the personnel cost, and so on.

How Repairs Are Charged

At this point the question arises: who will be charged for the repair? This is decided by the school district or organization, and may be different according to the locality or organization. Some maintenance department budgets comprise all repairs and alterations. In other organizations, those that tend to have site-based leadership, repair costs are charged back to individual building accounts. No matter where these costs are billed, they reflect the actual cost of the material, not the estimated cost, as well as the actual labor costs.

Some organizations use a formula, so that all costs are computed equitably. Such a formula may look like the following:

$$\text{Travel (from/to job)} + \text{Hours on the Job} \times \text{\# of Men} + \text{Parts} = \text{Cost of Job}$$

An additional 5 percent of the cost of the parts may be added for incidentals. These may be nuts, bolts, grease, oil, and other items that are not handled by inventory. Personnel costs are computed several ways as well. Often it is easier to charge a standard "shop" rate calculated on the total maintenance wages, plus the benefits. This rate needs to be recalculated periodically to reflect wage changes.

Reference

Note: A special note of thanks to Gloucester County Public Schools and its administrators, James Camp, Senior Director of Maintenance and Engineering, and Victor Hellman, Executive Director of Administrative Service and Finance, for assistance with the examples in this chapter.

CHAPTER 5

Capital Improvement and Maintenance Planning

Introduction

A school system staff normally uses a capital improvement program to provide safe and modern facilities for all students in a systematic fashion. A capital improvement program addresses the need for equitable facilities throughout the school system and also serves as a means of providing the types and kinds of building students need for effective learning. The implied charge for the school board to help students learn effectively is carried out through the provision of good facilities.

The director of facilities in the local school system helps the school board realize that goal. That individual knows what quality in a building is and should be able to apply that knowledge through architectural and construction requirements. At the same time, the director of facilities must understand how school buildings play a role in student learning.

Capital Improvement Planning

Every school organization in the country needs to have an ongoing capital improvement program. This applies to both public and private schools. Even though a school organization may not construct a new school building on a regular basis, there are sufficient improvement needs to existing buildings to require a systematic capital improvement program. A capital improvement program can be considered a form of an action or work plan that emanates from the much larger long-range plan of the school system. The capital improvement program differs from a true action plan in that it covers the work of the facilities maintenance department for 5–7 years, whereas action plans stemming from the long-range plan usually have a life of one year.

41

The result of the major planning activities of the school staff is the Long-Range Plan. Sometimes this is called the Strategic Plan, the Comprehensive Plan, the Six-Year Plan, the Master Plan, or the Educational Development Plan. All of these terms have been used to describe the systematic plan to be followed by the entire school system for 3–5 years. The Long-Range Plan is normally developed system-wide after considerable planning efforts by a large number of individuals both inside and outside the school organization.

The Long-Range Plan serves as the document for all individuals within the school system to work towards common goals. The LRP addresses the goals of the school system, the recipients of the services, and the resources available. This document's concepts, however, are never intended to be implemented in and of themselves. The LRP contains an excess of data relative to the needs of the school organization. The forward movement of the school system is described on several fronts in that document, which addresses the work of all departments of the school organization. Because of the enormity of the data and the scope of the planning statements, the work entailed in implementing the LRP is devolved to smaller documents. The documents that actually serve as the implementation tools are called Action Plans or Work Plans.

Action Plans

The actual implementation of the Long-Range Plan is done through the various Action Plans (Earthman, 2000). The LRP permeates the entire school organization, and each department and school building has a certain responsibility for implementing a portion. All major departments or offices of the school system are involved in the work of implementing Action Plans. Figure 5.1 illustrates the relationships among the Long-Range Plan, various Action Plans, and the individuals responsible for implementation. As can be seen in Figure 5.1, these responsibilities cover the entire spectrum of the functions of the school system.

The exact format of the Action Plans may vary, but each plan should address the: (1) work to be completed, (2) objectives of the job, (3) measures of effectiveness, (4) costs needed to attain the objectives, and (5) deadlines for completion. Action Plans might also address further division of work by smaller organizational units, the quality of the product that is needed, and sources of assistance available. Action Plans may also contain statements regarding limitations, handicaps, and constraints the department may have to overcome.

One important part of the Action Plan is the resources needed to complete the objectives. These resources are usually in the form of personnel, time, and funds. Such resource allocation is in the form of department, office, school site, or individual budgets that are derived from the general operational budget of the

Large-range Plan Section	Type of Action Plan	Responsibility
(1) Community Characteristics		
(2) Educational Plan Description		
Present Plan:	Curriculum Development	Director of Curriculum
Proposed Plan:	Instructional Development	Director of Instruction
	Human Resource Plan	Director of Human Resources
(3) Student Projections	Demographic Study for SDE Funding	Director of Research
(4) Facility Needs	Capital Improvement Plan	Director of Facilities
(5) Financial Plan	Budgetary Plans	Director of Finance
	Operating Budget	
	Capital Budget	
	Annual School Site Plan	Principal & Staff

Figure 5-1 Action Plans.

school system. In the case of the capital improvement plan, there may also be resources derived from the capital budget.

The life of an Action Plan is usually one year following the life of the operational budget. In each succeeding year, new Action Plans are developed in accordance with the accomplishments of the most recent Action Plan. The work of an Action Plan that was not accomplished in one year is carried over into the new Action Plan, to form a part of it. When there is a change of priorities, certain items may be dropped or reassigned to different years. Such changes are not a negative reflection on the Long-Range Plan, but rather the recognition that the Plan is a living document that changes according to needs.

The data in the Long-Range Plan regarding the physical facilities is obtained through a detailed inspection and evaluation of all the physical property owned and operated by the school system. As part of the process of obtaining data for the LRP, individuals experienced in evaluating school buildings visit and evaluate all buildings. The results of these evaluations are compiled into the LRP, and recommendations or needs are then expressed. The evaluations address the needs to maintain or improve the existing facilities as well as any possible needs for new facilities. The section of the LRP dealing with facilities must take into account possible growth or decline of the student body, changes in the educational programs offered, and the natural deterioration and wearing of existing buildings.

Definition of Maintenance and Capital Improvement

The compilation of building needs may include what would normally be called maintenance items and capital improvement items. This mixture of projects must at one point in time be separated into the two different types of projects. The difference between maintenance items and capital improvement projects is not a clearly defined line. Nevertheless, there is a division. The main difference between maintenance projects and capital improvement projects is the manner in which the individual projects are funded. Projects that cost more than what can be accommodated within the annual operating budget are termed *capital improvement projects*. Such projects are usually funded with borrowed revenue. Projects that can be funded within the annual operating budget are identified as maintenance items. This arbitrary method of classification is used widely throughout school organizations. The size of the project is also a consideration as to whether or not it is classified as a maintenance item. The definition of maintenance work is any work or action that keeps a building in a state of good repair, functioning properly, and as near the original condition as possible (Earthman, 1994). These actions or projects range from repairing windows to re-roofing. For the most part, these activities do not in a formal sense, enhance or improve the structure beyond the building's original design.

Capital Improvement Program

The specific Action Plan of interest here is the capital improvement program, which is developed by those individuals responsible for school facilities. The CIP is also referred to as the capital improvement plan. The capital improvement program (CIP) is a set of proposed actions to provide appropriate housing for the students enrolled in the school system (Castaldi, 1994). The main difference between the Action Plans of say the Human Resources Department or the Curriculum Department and the CIP is that the CIP usually extends for 5–7 years, a time-frame determined by the number of projects and their extended completion times.

The capital improvement program always contains more projects than the school system has funds to complete. As a result, each project is prioritized according to its importance to the proper housing of students in safe and modern buildings. Many factors enter into the prioritizing of each project, and many individuals participate in the process. The exact timing of each project is determined by cooperative action on the part of numerous individuals. The superintendent or head of the school organization in the private sector, plus the financial officer must be involved. In small organizations, the school board or board of trustees may even be involved in prioritizing the projects to be considered.

The actual capital improvement program document lists every project that will be accomplished using capital funds normally derived from the sale of

Project B0156
Jefferson High School

Description: A project is required to plan and construct a 60-station high school in the northern Oakbridge area to be completed by the year 2004.

Justification: Rapid residential housing construction in the area to be served has required construction of five schools in the last four years. Enrollments are projected to increase in the next five years.

Expenditure Schedule (000's)

Cost Element	Total	2000	2001	2002	2003	2004
Plan/Design	1,200	270	700	100	90	40
Land	900	900				
Site Improvement	500		500			
Construction	20,280			20,280		
Furniture/Equipment	1,900					1,900
Total	24,780	1,170	1,200	20,380	90	1,940

Figure 5-2 Capital Project Description.

bonds, which are paid off through funds in the operational budget. Each project, no matter how large or small, is listed with a complete description of what will be done and where it will be completed. For example the simplest project listing might be for a new school at a certain location, which would require only two-three sentences to describe. The most complicated project description might be of a renovation. In some cases, there may be a statement justifying a project. The estimated cost of the project and the scheduled time of completion are also provided. The cost data may be broken out according to the various elements of the project such as planning, construction, land acquisition, and furniture and equipment. Figure 5.2 illustrates a possible capital improvement program project as listed in the document.

Determining Costs

The cost for each project must cover all possible expenditures. In the example in Figure 5.2, the costs associated with planning, design, construction, site acquisition, and furniture and moveable equipment are detailed. In some manner, the school system staff must determine how much each part of the project will cost and in turn the total cost of the project. Determining costs can be done in several ways, but regardless of the calculations, past data must be used as a basis of judgment for the future. Therefore, the calculation of the cost of a project results from previous similar projects and are basically estimates.

The most common figure used in planning facility projects is the square foot cost. The square foot cost of a building is derived by dividing the total square footage contained in the building into the total cost of the building. The total cost of the building includes change orders executed during construction, furniture and moveable equipment, and site and development costs, in addition to the contract cost of construction. The total building cost can be contrasted with a cost of the building alone. This latter figure excludes the costs of furniture, equipment, site acquisition, and development. Building costs alone are calculated by dividing the total square footage into the contracted cost of the building. As can be seen, both cost figures are useful indices in planning projects.

Many state departments of education require school systems to report cost figures to them. The department of education staff then compiles all of these data and determines average costs throughout the state. These figures are useful to the local school system to help in their planning efforts. Such data are public information and as such can be obtained and used by private/parochial schools to help in their planning for capital projects. A certain amount of caution must be exercised in some states that have large metropolitan school systems, if data from these areas are included in the average square foot cost figures. Normally in such cases, there are separate averages for metropolitan and non-metropolitan areas.

Architectural firms that specialize in the design of school buildings have a rich data bank on previous work in a great many different areas. These firms are excellent sources of information relative to building costs. Architects can be called on to assist a small school system devise cost figures for capital projects. These same architectural firms have cost figures broken down into components of a school, even to the classroom level. It is not unheard of for an architect to be able to tell a school system how much it would cost to construct a wall, lay a floor of a certain type, the cost to install a ceiling, or the installation of a window. These rather detailed cost figures assist the architect in the design of the building and can assist school systems in their planning for capital improvements. These cost figures are helpful in completing the capital improvement program and are in almost all cases very current. Costs associated with the purchase of furniture or equipment can easily be obtained through any reputable vendor at no obligation and can be used for budgetary purposes.

In some cases, school organizations need to purchase land for a new building or an expansion of an existing building. For planning purposes, school systems must know how much they will need to spend on a parcel of land. The source for such figures can be found in the county or municipal governmental offices. The purchase price of all land transactions must be registered with the local government. These data can be helpful in determining land values and fair price.

The capital improvement program normally contains more projects than the school system can afford to complete in one year. As a result, the projects are prioritized according to the needs of the school system. Each project is then listed in the appropriate year in which it is to be funded. Thus, projects are listed in every year of the capital improvement program, which is usually 5-7 years. Each year contains a listing of projects the school system expects to fund during that year. In the case of large projects, funds may be committed over a space of several years before the project is completed. In the case of a renovation project, the furniture and moveable equipment will not be needed before the project is completed. As a result, funds for the furniture and equipment are provided at the close of the project.

Capital Improvement Budget

In order to complete the capital improvement program, the projects contained therein must be initiated serially according to the years of the program. In other words, the CIP must be broken down into manageable funded projects, according to the annual and long-term resources of the school organization. The projects listed in the first year of the CIP then become the capital improvement proposed budget for that year. This is the final working plan or Action Plan of the facilities department.

A budget of any type is an approved plan of expenditures, revenues, and objectives. The objectives of the capital improvement budget are the listed projects to be completed. The expenditures are the costs associated with each project, and the revenues are the sources of funds to complete the project.

The governing body of the school organization must formally approve both the capital improvement program and budget. The capital improvement program is the general prioritized listing of projects to be completed using borrowed funds. This document covers activities spanning from 5 to 7 years. But adoption of the program does not give the school staff any authority to do anything on these projects. The real authority for initiating a project is through the approved capital improvement budget. Usually a proposed capital improvement budget is offered to the governing body of the school organization. Upon approval, the document becomes the official budget that authorizes school staff to begin expending funds. This is the authority for action and the expenditure of funds by the school staff.

With this authorization, the school staff can begin contracting for work and services, the purchase of material, and acquisition of furniture and equipment. In other words, the staff can begin those activities associated with initiating projects for that year.

Project Classification

All maintenance projects can be defined into four categories: (1) long-range maintenance (2) annual projects, (3) short-term projects [SB 5.1 and 5.2], and (4) emergency repairs and maintenance. Every maintenance plan should have items in these categories. Some larger school systems will have projects in all categories in their maintenance budget each year. Items such as a roof replacement, new boiler, and replacement of lighting systems might be considered projects that should be funded through the use of capital or borrowed funds. The annual projects usually result from the yearly inspection of the building conducted by the principal, custodian, and central office personnel. These projects or items should be funded through the annual operational budget. Items under this category might include painting, ceiling repairs, reconditioning of floors, and restroom fixture replacement. The short-term maintenance projects might include a door replacement, minor tune-up of motors, and removal of a wall. The last category includes emergency repairs needed to keep the school functioning efficiently. Since emergencies cannot be known in advance, projects in this category are budgeted using a special contingency fund.

Major maintenance projects are different from projects designed to repair parts of the building by restoring systems. Repairing a part of the building keeps the structure in good condition so those users of the building can function in a safe and efficient environment. Usually, repair items are small in nature and result from failure of a system or structure. These types of projects are usually completed by the maintenance staff and may or may not be included in the capital improvement program. Typically these items are reported by the principal of the school on emergency repair forms and completed by the various craft and trades personnel employed by the school system.

References

Castaldi, B. (1994, 4th edition). *Educational facilities: Planning, modernizion, and Management.* Needham, MA: Allyn and Bacon, Inc.

Earthman, G. I. (2000). *Planning educational facilities for the next century.* Reston, VA: Association of School Business Officials, International.

Earthman, G. I. (1994). *Renovation handbook: Investing in education.* Lancaster, PA: Technolics Publishers, Inc.

CHAPTER 6

Cost of Maintenance

Maintenance Formulas

DETERMINING the amount of budgetary funds for maintenance work can be done in many ways. The amount of maintenance funds in the budget may reflect a very rational approach to needs or may be a more informal estimate. Some budget numbers may seem like there is no relationship between maintenance needs of buildings and the amount allocated in the budget. In other situations, the allocation may appear to be based upon a very real effort to address maintenance needs.

The formulation and approval of the budget of the local school system, whether public or private, is a politically charged activity. Regardless of the orientation of the school system, decision-makers have differing thoughts and beliefs about how the school should operate, spend funds, and maintain buildings. These differences must be resolved before the budget can be formulated and approved. Most differences of opinion regarding the budget center on parts that deal with personnel and curriculum, the sections where most of the funds are allocated.

Maintenance Allocation

There are several ways to determine how funds are allocated for maintenance work, ranging from guesswork to the use formulas. In some school systems, the amount of funds proposed for the maintenance section of the budget is determined by how much was spent the previous year. This amount is then entered into the proposed budget for the next year. In some cases, the amount from previous years is increased a certain percent to reflect inflation. This method of determining a budget amount for maintenance assures the governing board there are no surprises. The gradual increase in funds simply permits the maintenance department to stay current with costs, if the amount of the increase truly reflects inflation. In other words, the increase may or may not reflect reality. The increase may reflect political reality rather than true increases in costs of maintenance. This method of determining the total amount of funds to be requested in the budget leaves much to be desired. In the first place, the amount of funds in the previous budget may or may not reflect the actual needs of caring for the buildings in the school system. If it does not, then the school system is routinely underfunding building maintenance, which can lead to accelerated deterioration and higher future outlays. For instance, at the end of 50 years a building may be in much worse condition than it should be, and the school system will be required to spend a proportionately greater outlay to bring the building back to its original shape. Where schools use the "prior year" method of allocating funds, it is important for administrators to examine whether the allocation is in fact sufficient to maintain the facilities.

Allocation Formulas

Formulas also can be used to determine the amount of funds requested for the proposed operating budget. The development of formulas is based on the need to keep a building in as good a state of repair as possible. These formulas have been developed based upon the determination of real needs of buildings over a period of years using a scientific approach. Three major criteria are used in a formula to determine the amount of maintenance funds to be allocated in the operating budget: (a) percentage of the total general operational budget; (2) percentage of the total replacement cost of the school building and equipment, (3) cost of maintenance based upon square footage. Each of these formulas has advantages and disadvantages, but all reflect a rational approach to proper funding of maintenance projects.

Some school systems rely upon allocating a certain percentage of the general operational budget for maintenance work. This formula is simple, but is in effect similar to the "prior year" method. Calculated funds may or may not reflect actual needs. The percentage of school budgets devoted to maintenance projects has decreased gradually over the past 80 years. In 1920, approximately 14.1 percent of the local school operational budget was devoted to the maintenance section. That percentage decreased until approximately 6.7 percent of the general operational budget of the local school system was devoted to maintenance projects in1982 (Honeyman & Sayles, 1999). Currently, the amount of the operational budget devoted to maintenance approaches 4 percent. There are many reasons for this drop in the percentage of funds dedicated to maintenance work. The most important being the significant overall increase in the amount of the budget devoted to personnel costs. The total impact of these costs can reach 80 percent of the total operational budget. The fact that the school staff in the early part of the century did not have recourse to a retirement system, health insurance, and other benefits that they do today speaks to this increase. The increases in energy costs have also impacted the budget, along with inflationary trend over the years. If these inflationary elements are factored, the real portion of the budget devoted to maintenance is more stable than it appears. However, the percentage of a line item compared to the overall total is important in a budget, since often an item that receives proportionally less is deemed less important and more liable to be reduced.

In cases of budget reductions, the maintenance section is one of the first to be reduced because there are no parents or teachers at the budget hearing to resist the cut or advocate. The gradual deterioration of the percent of funds maintenance can claim in the operational budget is distressing to the administrators and detrimental to the condition of the school buildings. Budget cuts are one cause of the deplorable conditions affecting many public schools buildings, as documented by various governmental agencies and professional organizations.

The use of a formula that ties maintenance costs to a percentage of the replacement costs of a building is popular with various governmental agencies, as well as school systems. This formula provides for an amount to be spent each year in keeping the building in a state of good repair. The formula has proved quite successful, but has not been put to great use in school systems throughout the country. The United States Navy uses a factor of 3 percent of the total replacement cost of the building each year as the amount of funds needed for each building. The formula uses the established replacement cost of the building and multiplies that figure by 3 percent. The resulting amount of funds should then be devoted to keeping the building in a state of good repair. Over a thirty-five year period, an amount equal to over 100 percent of the replacement cost of the building has been applied to maintaining the building in good shape. After thirty-five years, the building is in line for a major remodeling or rehabilitation.

Some progressive school systems allocate each year an amount that represents 2 percent of the replacement cost of the buildings for maintenance projects of every sort. The replacement cost is determined by an appraisal of the worth of the building, usually done by either local school system employees or an appraiser from the insurance industry. That figure is used to apply the 2 percent formula to determine fund requests. An elementary school building that had a replacement cost of approximately $5 million would then need a fund allocation of approximately $100,000 per year for maintenance projects. After 50 years, an amount equal to the total replacement cost of the building has been spent to keep the building in good repair. After the fiftieth year, the building is scheduled for a major project to replace all of the major systems and renovate the structure.

The California Department of Education recommends a percentage of no less than 2.9 percent of the total replacement cost of the building and equipment.

This amount does not provide for "catch-up" needs (CDOE, 1986). A percentage of the total replacement value of the buildings and equipment is related to the amount of property to be maintained and is automatically adjusted for changes in labor and material costs each year. This formula is probably the best measure for establishing maintenance allocations for a proposed budget.

The third formula used to develop budgetary figures links the costs of maintenance and square footage. Under this formula, the square footage in a building is multiplied by a factor representing the total cost of all maintenance projects approved the previous year. If the school system has a number of schools, the average cost of all projects in the system is factored into the average. The average is then divided into the total square footage of all buildings in the system. The resultant factor is than applied to the total square footage of all buildings. The product of this arithmetical expression is then the maintenance dollar allocation inserted into the operating budget for the coming year. Consider a school system with 8 buildings that have a total of 840,000 square feet of space in all buildings. Assume the average dollar cost of the maintenance projects for the past year was $200,000. When that amount is divided into the total square footage of all buildings, a factor of $4.70 is achieved. That factor represents the amount spent for maintenance per square foot of building space. This should be multiplied by the 840,000 square feet to arrive at a figure of $3.5 million to be placed in the operating budget for maintenance for the coming year.

Maintenance Reserve Fund

Some school systems establish a reserve fund to provide resources for extraordinary or emergency projects. The projects completed through such a fund are normally those that cannot be anticipated or planned for. When such projects occur, if a reserve fund is not available, they must be funded through the budgeted maintenance fund. The regularly budgeted maintenance funds must then be drained to complete the emergency work. The unanticipated claim on the maintenance funds then deprives other projects of funding. As a result, the work scheduled for the current year must be deferred to another year. Creating a maintenance reserve fund to take care of unexpected projects is good stewardship. The prudent administrator must recognize there are times when emergency or unanticipated events occur and plan for such situations. The reserve fund is the proper answer to this situation. The maintenance reserve fund should be a continuing fund that is earmarked for only such projects. Special policies regarding the proper use of such funds should be developed and approved by the school board.

In several states, the local school system cannot establish such a fund. In those states where the local school system cannot raise funds for its operation or is dependent upon another governmental unit to raise taxes, a reserve fund may not be legal. In other words, if a school system receives all of its local funding from another governmental unit, there is usually a provision that all moneys not spent within the budget year are returned to the proper governmental unit. There is no legal provision for a school board to carry over funds from one year to another. Often, there is an explicit prohibition against this.

There are several methods for determining the amount of funds to set aside for a reserve fund. The most obvious method is to determine the amount of funds that were used in emergencies over the past ten years. The mean dollar amount of these funds is a starting point for establishing the reserve fund. Another measure might be an estimate of the cost for replacing a roof, a boiler, or electrical system in the average school building. These cost estimates would provide a good foundation for the reserve fund; however, initially the amount of these expenditures would not equal the total needs.

There are formulas that can be used to establish a reserve fund. These formulas endeavor to rationalize a system of determining the amount of funds required. Maintenance work covers the areas of building condition, equipment, and grounds. All three factors require attention in the normal work schedule of the maintenance department. Therefore, the cost needs within these three areas must be factored into any formula used.

The California Department of Education (1986) has developed a formula that produces the needed funds for building maintenance, equipment repair and replacement, and the upkeep of grounds. The first part of the formula determines the replacement costs of the buildings. This is done by multiplying the total square footage of all buildings in the school system by a cost factor developed by the state. This factor is the mean cost of all building projects approved the previous year by the Department of Education. The resultant product is the total replacement value of all buildings. The second calculation is done by multiplying the total replacement cost of the building by a factor of 1.8 percent. The product represents the amount of funds for the building repair reserve.

The needed funds for equipment repair for the reserve fund is determined by using values of the total replacement cost of buildings. Equipment values are equal to 11 percent of the cost of buildings; this would be the value of equipment replacement. In addition, the repair of equipment equals 5 percent of the equipment replacement costs. Thus, the building replacement costs found in the previous calculations would be multiplied by 11 percent to establish equipment replacement costs. The replacement costs are then multiplied by 5 percent to obtain the equipment repair needs reserve.

The equipment replacement costs are developed by using the equipment values determined above, which is 11 percent of the total replacement cost of all buildings. The equipment replacement cost is multiplied by 3.33 percent to obtain the annual reserve needed for replacement of equipment. The

3.33 percent figure is derived from the useful life of equipment, which is 30 years.

The formula to determine the annual need for grounds upkeep uses the total square feet of all buildings multiplied by the cost per square foot for repair of buildings. The product of this calculation is multiplied by 5 percent, and this represents the multiplier for the total square feet of grounds. The last calculation is to multiply the total square feet of grounds by 5 percent to arrive at the annual reserve needed for upkeep of grounds.

The four products of these calculations are summed to obtain the total annual maintenance reserve fund needed.

Repair of Buildings	$ _____
Repair of Equipment	$ _____
Replacement of Equipment	$ _____
Upkeep of Grounds	$ _____
Total Annual Maintenance Reserve Fund	$ _____

The formula for determining maintenance funds to be included within revenue limits and reserves to be raised begins with the percent of the operating budget spent for all maintenance in the previous year and uses that as a multiplier on the current operating budget. The product is the amount of maintenance funds to be included within the operating budget for each year. The next calculation subtracts the total annual maintenance reserve needed from the maintenance reserves included within the operating budget. The result is the additional amount of maintenance reserve to be raised for an adequate program.

The formulas are presented in graphic form in the Appendix. A simple step-by-step explanation is provided. All of the formulas use a percentage factor of the total cost to replace the current inventory of buildings and equipment owned by the school system. Data from previous building projects are used to develop the various percentages used in the formulas. These percentages represent how much of the project was accounted for by the factors. In other words, previous budgets and expenditures from those budgets form the bases of the percentages. The percentages represent the amount of funds actually spent for repairs to buildings and equipment in the previous year. The percentage used for equipment replacement is a simple calculation based upon the life of equipment. The formulas use a very rational approach to determining the appropriate amount of funds that will be needed in the future. For the school administrator, such formulas can be presented cogently to the school board and community, because they represent in concrete dollar terms what might be called optimum building maintenance.

References

California State Department of Education. (1986). *Administration of maintenance of operations in California school districts.* Sacramento, CA: Division of School Facilities and Transportation.

Honeyman, D. S. and Sayles, K. (1999). *The condition of America's schools.* Gainesville, FL: University of Florida, Center for the Study of Education Finance in Florida. EF 005 151.

CHAPTER 7

Deferred and Preventative Maintenance

A maintenance job or project identified as needing to be completed and scheduled and that has not been completed within the year scheduled can be classified as a deferred maintenance item. If the deferred item is completed within the next budget year, it is no longer a deferred item. When many maintenance projects or jobs are deferred from one year to the next in succession, administrators usually refer to that backlog of projects as the deferred maintenance program. In essence, those projects do not form any kind of a program or schedule. On the contrary, these projects are in reality a backlog of work that needs to be done and should have been done at the proper time. This situation is similar to that of the homeowner who puts off the outside painting of the house beyond when it should be completed or the repair of a loose door or replacement of a worn out fan in the bathroom. In the homeowner's definition, these items constitute the deferred projects that need to be completed. It is convenient to refer to this backlog with the euphemism, the deferred maintenance program.

Deferred Maintenance Programs

The idea of a program connotes that there is a planned deferral of selected projects. Planning is seldom involved. In some cases, school administrators may earmark projects that will be deferred in the event the full budget request is not approved. In those cases, certain projects are dropped from the list to be presented in the budget for the following year to the school board.

Deferring a maintenance project to the following year is not bad in and of itself, as long as the project is funded in a reasonable time. The continued deferring of projects over a number of years, however, results in an excessive backlog. The larger the backlog of projects, the more funds are needed to eliminate the backlog. Thus, a backlog can be seen as a kind of prelude to a budget deficit. Habitual deferring of projects can cause severe repercussions to both the quality of the existing buildings and to the capacity of the school organization to begin new projects. With a large backlog of projects and jobs, the school system is forced into continual prioritizing, a no-win situation for the school system, since the administration cannot properly address normal deterioration, along with the increasing backlog.

Deferred Maintenance Causes

Deferred maintenance backlogs often grow due to a lack of available funds to complete all needed work. For the past 20 years, school boards have been seeing school budgets increase slowly in relation to the expressed needs of the educators and the educational program. At budget reviews prior to the approval process, school boards and administrators must wrestle with the budget limitations imposed by either other governmental units or tax increases. Each year the school board must set a tax rate that is acceptable to the general public and at the same time include increases to accommodate growth or changes in the educational program. This tightrope act is extremely difficult for the school board and school administrators and results in some risk taking on the part of all. The demands from the teachers union or association for increases in salary are very difficult to ignore in the face of possible loss of faculty members or teacher demonstrations. At the same time, there are the normal demands of increased costs of materials, goods, and services that are necessary for the continued operation of the school system. These demands cannot be postponed.

All of these factors contribute to the situation where the needs of the maintenance program are not fully met. The actions of the school board regarding limitation or reduction of funds available to the maintenance program then lead to a backlog of maintenance projects. If such actions are taken year after year, the number of maintenance projects that have been deferred increases measurably. Maintenance directors then must face the dilemma of prioritizing projects year after year to assure those projects most crucial to health and safety receive priority.

Maintenance Mismanagement

Having a large deferred maintenance program does not result from mismanagement on the part of the school administrators. Rather, it results from a political decision made by the school board as a result of decreased public funds. The budgetary decision rests upon the perceptions of the school board members regarding what kind of a tax increase is acceptable and what is not acceptable. The tax rate level is perhaps the critical factor in a budget increase. Since it is rare for budgets to go down, it is rare that boards do not have to consider levying an increase. However, to increase the tax rate too much impacts the business and commercial interests of the community. Declining business or lack of local investment can seriously jeopardize the future growth of the community. The resultant downturn in the local economy further affects the ability of the community to produce the needed tax revenue. This downward cycle can continue if in the eyes of the community local taxes remain high. Few communities experience this kind of severe economic downturn, but many communities suffer from a high rate of taxation to provide the kinds of services, both educational and governmental, that are needed.

Obviously, it is much easier to get into an overloaded deferred maintenance program than it is to get out. Although there may be several strategies for school boards to take to address a large deferred maintenance program, they all involve a bootstrap type of effort. The school board must find additional funds to complete all of the projects in the backlog and at the same time maintain the progress of the school organization with no discernable reduction in program funds. This sort of action sounds simple, and even easy, to complete. The only problem is that finding additional funds to take care of all deferred maintenance projects at one time is virtually impossible.

Deferred Maintenance Costs

The costs to the schools of deferring maintenance items can be staggering. The true costs of deferring maintenance items are never properly identified because the natural deterioration of the building cannot be accurately measured, only estimated. Proper maintenance practices should help to keep the deterioration to a minimum, but deferring certain maintenance accelerates the normal deterioration.

The American Association of School Administrators published some of the earliest estimates of the cost of deferred maintenance throughout the country. The publication of The Maintenance Gap by the AASA, the Council of Great City Schools, and the National School Board Association identified the need to bring schools up to standard was approximately $25 billion (AASA, 1983). The survey included a population of 100 school districts throughout the country. The school districts ranged in size from New York City with over 1000 buildings and one million students and an annual expenditure of $3.2 billion in operating funds to a small school district in Tennessee with a budget of slightly under $5.0 million. The school districts in this survey spent an average of 6.7 percent of their annual budget for maintenance purposes. The $25 billion figure is approximately 20 years old and if increased by inflationary trends and new maintenance needs would escalate from 5 to 6 times that figure. The school districts identified 14 major areas in need of immediate repair. The most frequently mentioned area was repair or replacement of roofs.

Since that time there have been several studies investigating the condition of and maintenance needs of schools throughout the nation. Each successive study reports a higher sum of funds needed for deferred maintenance items. A major report conducted by the US General Accounting Office in 1995 (GAO, 1995) reported the results of a study on the condition of schools. This report announced a need of over $112 billion in repairs. That figure would include $11 billion of items needed to comply with federal regulations concerning provisions of the Americans with Disabilities Act and other governmental policies.

The National Center for Educational Statistics reported that about three-quarters of the school buildings in the United States would need repairs of various types (NCEF, 2000). This amounted to about 59,450 buildings in need of some repairs. The total cost of these repairs would amount to an estimated $127 billion in unbudgeted funds. The repairs to these buildings would average approximately $2.2 million for each school building and represent a per pupil cost of $3,900 for every student in the public schools regardless of whether or not the school building was included in the number of schools above that reported needing repairs. The report also stated that the emphasis upon new construction has drained away some of the funds that would have been used on maintenance.

The actual cost of deferred maintenance is difficult to compute because of many factors, one of which is the natural deterioration of the building. In addition, when maintenance is deferred, natural deterioration increases exponentially. For example, when a compromised roof is not properly repaired in a timely fashion, water can leak into areas where furniture and equipment can be destroyed and the carpet damaged. The leaking roof then precipitates other repairs, and the cost to bring the building up to standard increases greatly. In addition, repair costs increase due to inflation.

Unfortunately, the costs of deferred maintenance keep climbing; moreover, they are not felt uniformly. Honeyman and Sayles investigated the costs for maintenance repairs and replacement of buildings (1990). They developed a Replacement Cost Index for each building in the school districts in the survey, to provide data relative to the ability to finance a replacement. The index was compared to the sources of capital funds used for construction and maintenance in each district. The school districts that were least able to raise funds were the school districts that had the greatest repair and replacement needs. Although every school district in the survey was suffering from a severe backlog of maintenance needs, certain school districts felt the pinch of funds more acutely. This inequity of financial ability and needs is exacerbated in rural and small school districts, because of their limitations of resources supporting each student, small numbers of students, and debt limitation measures enacted by the states.

Most authorities recommend 2 percent of the replacement costs be spent on maintenance work each year in the life of the building. When less than that amount is spent, deferred maintenance occurs and accumulates each year, until the accumulated projects must be completed through some type of bootstrap operation such as a bond issue. Deferred maintenance in this instance can be classified as deficit budgeting, in that there is an accumulation of spending needs not accomplished. Many times the deferred maintenance projects are big-ticket items requiring considerable outlay of funding, perhaps more than the school system can afford in one year. To alleviate this, a maintenance reserve fund should be started

One of the first steps in budgeting for deferred maintenance projects is to complete an assessment of all capital investments, so that the expenditures necessary to restore buildings and equipment to the original condition can be projected. This assessment must identify all deferred maintenance items that must be completed. Following the assessment, the cost of each deferred maintenance project needs to be determined. The cost of deferred maintenance must take into account inflation during the life expectancy of the building. To calculate the deferred maintenance of a roof, for example, one must multiply the original cost of the roof by one plus the estimated inflation rate raised to the power equal to the life expectancy of the structure in years (Pitillo, 1993). The result of this calculation will be the replacement cost of the roof. For example, the initial cost of a roof might be somewhere in the neighborhood of $200,000. Assuming a life expectancy of 20 years for the roof and a projected rate of inflation of 3 percent for every year, the replacement cost in 20 years would be somewhere around $361,222. The inflationary increase in the replacement cost is compounded for each year, resulting in the amount above.

Assume one wants to determine the amount of deferred maintenance for a period of 5 years. To do this, one would divide the replacement cost by 20 and then multiply by 5 to find out that at the end of 5 years the deferred maintenance will amount to $90,306 (Pittillo, 1993). The formula for this is included in the sidebar.

$$\frac{200,000(1+0.03)_{20}}{20} \times 5 = \$90,306$$

Deferred Maintenance-Private and Parochial

Public schools across the country are experiencing a larger than desired deferred maintenance schedule, and the prospects for erasing the maintenance deficit are daunting. The same assessment can be made for private and parochial school organizations. The mountain of maintenance needs will continue to grow unless serious steps are taken to eliminate this backlog. For the public schools this will mean larger allocations of funds from the operating budget. It might also mean a program of debt funding over a period of years. In either case, there will need to be new sources of revenue tapped from the users of the school.

For the private and parochial sector, the remedy may mean increases in tuition payments, a capital fund drive, or increased subsidies from both religious and non-religious organizations to help raise the necessary funds to complete the deferred maintenance projects. Raising funds for special purposes is not an easy task in the private sector because of the limited population the schools serve. Parochial schools are also limited in fund raising by small congregations and student population. These school organizations, however, benefit from the larger church body, which has more resources than the local congregation.

Preventative Maintenance

The heading of this section could read, "What is the cost of not conducting preventative maintenance?" Too often school systems build a facility, install a new heating and ventilation system, or purchase a new and expensive piece of equipment and hope that it lasts forever. In the political processes of school district governance, it is too easy to remember large expenditures and budget for them, while failing to include in the following year's budget the upkeep for the facility or equipment. It is difficult to explain and convince the funding sources that equipment and systems are only as reliable as the least reliable part or component. Murphy's law is active to provide the greatest impact of such failures.

What is preventative maintenance?

Preventative maintenance is a planned program of care designed to prevent wear and tear on equipment, systems, or any operational facility components. This maintenance is scheduled to keep sudden breakdowns or failures from occurring and interrupting the services provided by the support operation. Such failures result in financial impact, both personnel costs and expenses related to the equipment, systems, parts, and health and safety. There may be a risk of personal harm, injury to maintenance employees and operators, or perhaps exposure to faulty equipment or exposure to certain chemicals if proper maintenance is not assured.

Preventative maintenance should be an organized process to prevent more than normal "wear and tear" on a piece of equipment, component, system, or facility. It assists in protecting a school district's assets and increasing the life of expensive and hard-to-replace equipment. The following are a few reasons to encourage the maintenance supervisor to stress the importance of preventative maintenance with staff, the central office, and the school board.

(1) The uptime of equipment is maximized through preventative maintenance.

(2) The lifetime of a facility, piece of equipment, or mechanical system is optimized through preventative maintenance.

(3) Preventative maintenance helps to guard against unplanned outages of critical systems or machinery.

(4) There are times when a lack of preventative maintenance will allow other malfunctions or problems to go unnoticed (i.e., leaks that lead to structural damage of a facility).

As is evident, there are costs associated with preventative maintenance; however, inaction may cost more to the overall facility or in terms of the lifetime operating costs of equipment, especially in cases where a school cannot afford to replace major system components. The school district may be "penny wise and pound foolish."

How To Go about Preventative Maintenance (PM)

When the Department of Education in California wrote its manual for key factors in a maintenance program, twelve factors were identified as being key to success. Some of the more important steps were to: (1) identify the equipment and facilities needing maintenance; (2) determine their present status; (3) determine the resources, including personnel, to get the job done; (4) establish priorities; (5) develop schedules; and, (6) keep to the schedule and maintain appropriate records for the next budget cycle. Most of these steps seem too logical, and one believes that any organization follows such a program. However, when the budget crunch hits, it is easy for the leadership to see the "lack of a squeaking wheel" as a reason for cutting funds. Recently, one maintenance director noted that PM can save "tons of money," but it also takes money to establish such a program. She went on to say that it might require one or more additional persons in each craft. In other words, it takes money to save money.

Equipment That May Need Preventative Maintenance

The most effective way to begin the preventative maintenance list is to review the school district inventory. The inventory should provide the base for nearly all equipment, systems, installations, and facilities. It should include descriptive information on square footage, age, types of systems, types of construction and materials that will be included in the master file or in the database. Another important way to ascertain maintenance needs is to review the industrial standards of the equipment or system and to make sure that manufacturer recommendations are followed. This can be a cost factor if the equipment and systems have certain maintenance guidelines that must be documented and followed in order to maintain the warranty.

Not just equipment needs attention. It may be power washing decking or cleaning hot air ducts to rid them of mites, mold, and mildew. The maintenance chore may be as simple as cleaning a school zone sign and making sure that the settings correspond to the correct times for when the school day begins and ends.

It is a simple job, but of paramount importance for the safety of the students, as well as the general public.

Plans for preventative maintenance, some school organizations call the process planned maintenance, should not only be centered around the manufacturers' information and suggestions, but also past service records. Preventative maintenance may assist in identifying equipment that is faulty. When the budget season rolls around, the faulty equipment can be replaced with more reliable and service free parts, systems, and components. A list follows of some of the possible items that may be on a custodial, buildings, and grounds maintenance schedule, but it is by no means inclusive. Certain districts may contract out some of the preventative maintenance, while others have the skilled technicians to conduct the work in house.

(1) Any HVAC equipment, including any moving parts, lubrication, filters, and simple cleaning

(2) Maintenance equipment such as compressors, and power equipment

(3) School furniture

(4) Playground sites and apparatus

(5) Roofing, water, and sewer systems

(6) Pumps, lighting fixtures, emergency and clock systems, and any safety equipment or systems.

Again, this list is not complete, but keeping in mind that all facilities do not deteriorate at the same rate, some equipment is of better quality than others, and past quality maintenance will assist the support services department in developing a schedule that will meet the needs of the school facilities.

Keeping Good Records

Most systems and equipment, when installed, provide recommendations for maintenance, but even small school districts have more items to track than one supervisor or maintenance worker can remember: refrigerant systems, cleaning vents, fans, and filters, lubricating moving parts of equipment, routine replacement of belts, and the list goes on. Therefore, the maintenance department must develop a tracking system for all facilities and the related systems, along with major pieces of equipment. This may be a card and file system or, more likely, a computerized database that is linked to maintenance software.

A computerized system may be PC based or web-based. Larger school organizations are going to web-based programs, in order that access may be made at multiple sites. The computerized information includes:

(1) A work order and scheduling process for work to be done by date and a record of what has been done

(2) A schedule that maximizes employee time

(3) A program that plans future jobs, so that necessary replacement parts, products, and materials are available when needed

(4) A work order system that includes labor comments, downtime, plus a complete historical record of the work completed

(5) A record of equipment and system information to include, make, model, serial number, and location

(6) A system that provides information on work to be completed, estimated length of job, type of work, labor that is necessary, and planned down time.

Cost of Preventative Maintenance Systems

As one might imagine, the more sophisticated the system, the more it is going to cost. Creative, computer-knowledgeable maintenance directors or directors with technology experts in their district may be able to develop their own system with a spreadsheet program that they already have. On the other hand, the preventative maintenance system may be a part of a software package for maintenance systems that can cost hundreds or thousands of dollars. Such upper-end systems include many more options than tracking maintenance.

The key is to know one's school district and to get the program that will pro-

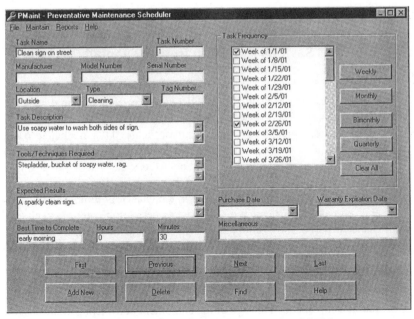

Figure 7-1 Sample Screen from Software Program - Scheduler.

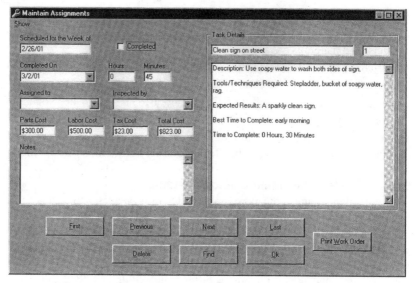

Figure 7-2 Sample Screen from Software Program - Assignments Screen.

vide the greatest service and meet the needs of the schools. Going the least expensive route may be more labor intensive and cost more money in the long run (CyberNiche).

Cost Savings Resulting from Preventative Maintenance Practices

The first cost factor that should be considered with preventative maintenance and keeping records of such is to assist in determining if equipment is uneconomical to operate. If breakdowns continue to occur and if the maintenance expenditures outweigh replacement costs, the equipment must be replaced. Preventive maintenance for an item should not exceed the cost of purchasing a new item.

A general rule of thumb is that the total maintenance program should consume approximately 5–7 percent of a district's operating budget. Preventative maintenance is part of the overall maintenance budget, and the exact portion is difficult to determine. Most certainly, the director must work to make sure that the preventative budget is less than the overall budget. To pinpoint the costs, however, the director must consider replacement costs, costs of downtime, loss of services, personnel, as well as normal depreciation. There is most probably a direct relationship between the age of the equipment or system and the cost of maintaining it. This cost projection is higher when the necessary preventative maintenance has not been conducted. If the department manager is monitoring the maintenance records and developing histories on all equipment and systems, it should be easier to ascertain at what point the equipment, facility, or system has provided its useful benefit. In addition, monitoring and replacement of this type can preclude catastrophic breakdowns.

Preventative maintenance may save more than the money needed to repair or replace equipment. It can do so by precluding injuries to operators of equipment or to students and employees who are near the equipment. It may prevent exposure to chemicals or dirty air, and/or it may prevent the loss of instructional time that is key to the success of our educators. Avoiding accidents saves money.

Facility Maintenance Considerations

Some school systems are concerned with "upfront costs" and do not consider the long-term maintenance component. Another important factor is whether or not maintenance over the life of a facility has been done in a timely manner. Was the roof replaced when it should have been? If not, was there structural damage? Was other maintenance deferred or was the building maintained well? Have the floors, exposed doors and windows, and other structural components received the attention necessary to keep the building safe and sound for the users? Finally, this schedule may be positively affected when major rehabilitations, renovations, and modernizations have occurred.

References

California State Department of Education. (1986). *Administration of maintenance of operations in California school districts.* Prepared under the direction of the School Facilities and Transportation Division.

CyberNiche Software. Retrieved May 21, 2002, from http://www.cniche.com/index.htm.

Pittillo, Robert A. (1993). Maintenance: The unavoidable. *Educational Facility Planner,* Vol 31, No. 4, pp 20–21.

CHAPTER 8

The Emerging Role of Technology in Facility Management and Maintenance

TECHNOLOGY—from computers to intranet services-represents a large advancement in facility management efficiency. Several reasons to incorporate technology into facility management and maintenance are:

(1) To provide better service to the students, employees, and public.
(2) To have greater accountability and have a record keeping system that exhibits this.
(3) To operate with greater efficiency in managing personnel, building systems, and inventory.

This chapter will elaborate the goals and benefits of applying technology systems to maintenance. At the same time, the point must be underscored that automated building systems should not be introduced too quickly and without the informed involvement of those who must learn and apply the technology. Technology is general, but each district's operating procedures are unique. Automated programs must be adapted to work within the guidelines of the district, not vice versa.

Integrating Facilities and Learning Through Technology: Automated Building Systems

Maintenance and engineering functions can be separated into five areas:

(1) Maintenance
(2) Operations
(3) Engineering

(4) Administration

(5) Staff development

For efficient and effective service, these five areas must mesh, which does not occur by accident. Without a plan, maintaining a building is a matter of survival-getting through just one more day. The services provided employees and students may or may not remain adequate and accurate. Definitely, the level and scope of alterations, maintenance, and repairs are not optimized. One of the ways to provide an efficient operation is to have a system that automates and tracks all five areas. An effective software system will synchronize and weave a network for the facility that will improve speed and efficiency of service, maintain appropriate inventories, optimize the use of personnel, decrease the vulnerability to disruption, and minimize unplanned downtime. The greatest advantage of having a well-developed automated building system is that it is cost effective. Another often overlooked advantage is the database of information that is developed and made accessible to a number of users.

Automated Building Systems

The automated building trend began in the 1960s when electronic controls evolved. Initially this was done through off-site mainframe computers, which allowed for zero control over the scheduling at the local level. For example, air conditioning had to be turned on from hundreds of miles away. The 1980s and 1990s brought the PC, and school districts and organizations began to develop their own digital controls for controlling HVAC operations. At the same time, costs declined.

So what does an automated building system entail? According to Coggan, "an intelligent [or automated] building combines innovations, technological or not, with skillful management, to maximize return on investment" (Coggan, 1999, p. 1). Many experts go on to say that it is a building that uses technology and personnel to provide energy efficient, safety systems, telecommunications systems, and workplace automation or instructional software. These four categories are integrated into one single computerized system. Thus, on one computer server there may be software present for the bell system of a school, the security system, the fire alarms, HVAC, e-mail, instructional applications, and so on.

Safety Systems

Automation has evolved rapidly in the area of safety. Many high schools today have closed-circuit television and other security systems. Identification cards with pictures, soft screens that recognize palms, and card access controls are a part of the security regimen. The database for some of these systems is housed on the school server or on an area server. Special controls have been developed for HVAC, doors, fire alarms, and elevators, so that if an emergency occurs, all systems can be controlled from a central area. The building administrator must assign someone to be in charge of these systems when an emergency occurs. During and after the Columbine High School shooting, no one had the authority to turn off the fire alarm. It rang for hours.

Computerized Maintenance Management Software (CMMS)

CMMS is an enabling technology (software) that integrates preventative maintenance, work order maintenance, inventory tracking, purchasing, tool crib management, energy management, lock and key control, assets, equipment repair histories, vendor histories, CAD drawings of facilities, personnel information, and many more areas. It may have a project manager component, tickler file for reminders on expiring contracts, a scheduler, a budget manager, a document manager, and so on. This software is the fiber that holds the operations and maintenance department together to improve effectiveness, efficiency, and reduce costs.

When looking for such a program, the maintenance director, along with the technology department, should take considerable time and methodically make a selection based on ease of use, friendliness of the software, affordability, ease of integration into existing systems, and how quickly the system can be deployed. Of greatest importance is to make sure that the software can be configured to meet the needs of the organization and is the latest technology as the department grows and is able to automate and computerize more procedures. Other key elements include the report capabilities of the software, regulatory compliance tracking, the integration of the system with municipal PCs and other programs of the organization, and the ongoing support given by the supplier.

Implementing a CMMS Program

CMMS software is only as good as the plan for its implementation and all of the activities that precede the installation. According to most software experts, a proper CMMS program should have a minimum of two databases ready prior to the installation: one is a complete inventory of all of the equipment of the custodial, maintenance, and engineering department, and the other is maintenance information that identifies all of the maintenance actions necessary for every item in the equipment inventory. These are needed for the maintenance operation to be able to generate valid work orders. Other databases may make the program more effective, such as CAD drawings of all of the facilities, but the inventory and service information are the minimum.

Inventory and service databases must be constructed with datasets in mind. For the inventory, these include regularly gathered information, such as cost of replacement, serial number, date purchased, location, vendor, place purchased, and other pertinent facts. There may be notes on a specific piece of equipment, such as downtime or safety problems. A list of maintenance actions should be correlated with the use of the inventoried equipment. Such a listing will include:

(1) Schedule of preventative maintenance for the equipment, along with regular servicing information

(2) History of maintenance and repairs on the equipment

(3) Consumable parts that may need to be inventoried or a list of vendors who can deliver such parts on short notice

(4) Information about what craft(s) may be necessary to repair equipment and if the department has someone trained to do so.

There also should be a procedure in the process that notes when the equipment is changed or removed from service.

Budget Implications

Most school divisions are being forced to do more with less. This is especially true of the maintenance departments. The maintenance teams are expected to provide superior professional service, meet all of the standards of the government and other regulatory bodies, deliver services within the least time possible, provide a system that exhibits accountability, and continually reduce the budget impact. For this to be accomplished, most managers see automation as a key factor. The front-end costs should be carefully projected and monitored. If these are controlled, the long-term benefits should provide a payback.

Maintaining an Up-to-Date System

After a software package is procured and implemented, it is only as good as the monitoring designed to determine whether the CMMS program continues to be effective. As the requirements of the maintenance and operations department change, so should the CMMS program. Early on, in the use of the software, the department needs to develop a mission and goals. One such goal may be to reduce downtime of equipment, develop meaningful reports that will assist in control, and maintain histories that will make the department more effective—information that will reveal the effectiveness of certain vendors and equipment.

A consideration when implementing the system should be provisions for updating the software and equipment. This is another reason to work closely with the technology department. Their expertise will ensure that updating provisions are a part of the budget, as well as part of the original contract, for the hardware and software.

Service Features

It has been noted that often the maintenance staff is overworked, underpaid, and earn a less than deserved reputation for not being sympathetic to the needs of the educators in the organization. A good CMMS program will assist in dispelling this reputation, as it enables the maintenance worker to shorten the response time, make necessary repairs or conduct the regular maintenance, and provide feedback to the initiator.

A good service program will offer an easy way for the administrator, usually the principal, to report a maintenance problem. Many times the reporting system is web-based and is a simple template asking for the location, identifying the problem, and providing any other descriptive information that is necessary for the maintenance worker to respond quickly. The work order automatically goes to the dispatcher, or in some cases the program has the capability of sending directly to the skills person who will make the service call. The same template allows the service worker to report the work performed and whether the problem was solved and will or will not need follow-up. The initiator of the problem is automatically notified for the repair and each step of the process. Finally, the program creates a record of the maintenance action and adds to the database to allow the administrators of the program to produce status reports. Thus, the program provides the building administrator, along with the other educators in the facility, with continual feedback that the problems they have are being responded to in a proper timeframe.

Energy Management Systems, Enterprise Energy Management

Energy Management Systems

In the beginning, energy management systems simply tracked energy use in an organization. During the budget process, facility managers could share with the department of budget and finance billing information and the amount of energy service needed. Advanced technology permitted better data management, along with the opportunity to develop energy management systems. These include utilities, both gas and electric, electrical equipment, and the impact of how equipment and services are scheduled and used. Computerized monitoring allows, too, for continuous review of data and automatic responses to the information that feeds into the system. The systems provide a greater understanding and control of energy costs, and they improve facility operations. Data is made available to prove whether or not certain projected savings are achieved.

A common energy management system controls HVAC units. Computers run and monitor the units 24/7. Each day may have a different schedule for heat or air conditioning-according to the daily use of the facility. This particular type of system in its early stages caused a great deal of concern, as a teacher could never stay late in a classroom without being without heat in the winter or air conditioning in the summer or without feeling uncomfortable when the HVAC schedule "kicked off" the climate control. Even with recent systems, problems can cause discomfort. It is extremely important for energy managers to explain to employees how the system works, how their needs will be met, and how the manager will respond to those needs.

However, energy management means more than monitoring and controlling HVAC. It entails:

(1) Starting and turning off equipment such as lighting, HVAC, and security operations on a set schedule

(2) Using computerized controls, optimizing the time that certain equipment is on (i.e., beginning to heat a facility only when it is necessary in order to reach a set temperature)

(3) Having large chillers and other equipment that use large amounts of electricity properly balanced, so unnecessary energy is not consumed

(4) Using outdoor air when possible for "free" heat or cooling

(5) Providing information for after-hours tenant billing

(6) Logging and reporting equipment failures for equipment histories-this is necessary to know effective alteration or replacement needs

(7) Coordinating indoor temperature settings to outdoor temperature;

(8) Coordinating the temperature settings to occupancy patterns

(9) Installing energy saving equipment, as replacements are necessary.

With a PC and the right program, there is no reason for a school organization, whether a large urban system or a small private school, not to have an energy management system working for them. If a more sophisticated system is desired, there is software that provides for the integration of this system to the security and fire system, as well as to coordinate multiple buildings in the organization. Energy management systems are claimed to save 10–20 percent of total energy costs.

Enterprise Energy Management (EEM)

EEM is a newer concept that has not been integrated into most educational facilities energy management plans. An EEM system can automatically confirm a problem with an energy source, can monitor any increase or curtailment in activities requiring energy, correlates billing data, and can initiate other energy sources when necessary. Most smaller school districts or private schools do not have a large enough energy usage to have an EEM plan. For example, in the 1990s, electricity was a great deal less expensive than it is today, and all-electric schools were built. In the southern part of the United States that may not be a problem, as the schools are in moderate temperature zones. However, in more northern states, as the cost of electricity has increased, the budgets of school are pinched. Some facility managers have installed large gas heating systems with computerized controls. When the outside temperature reaches a certain level, the computer system overrides the electrical heating system and initiates the gas burners to keep the school comfortable.

Schools have installed very sophisticated computer systems and any interruption in the power supply is damaging and costly. According to Energy User News, Oracle Corporation estimated that a reliable power supply is worth millions of dollars per hour. Computer chips worth thousands of dollars are damaged when there is an interruption in the power supply. Huge chillers cost many dollars more to operate when there is a power interruption. Therefore, school divisions are installing generators that can supply electricity to a single area (i.e., the computer room or the operations room) to be used when the traditional electricity grid fails to provide the necessary power.

The potential exists for power interruptions: storms, accidents, and power supplies that cannot keep up. Often the power supply is not steady; there are power surges and leaks that can damage equipment. Therefore, schools deploy on-site power sources by installing intelligent power meters and computerized controls that initiate them.

An EEM system usually consists of three components:

(1) Intelligent power meters installed at distribution points related to the equipment that needs continuous service
(2) Control software to operate the alternative systems
(3) Communication links for the meters and software, as well as a process to monitor the systems.

The advantages include preventing downtime, preventing equipment damage, and avoiding interruptions to instruction. Most importantly the EEM systems should result in cost savings.

Managing Telecommunications and Information Technologies

Today one is likely to find many telcom lines entering a school facility. This is a totally new area for which the maintenance department has responsibility.

Smaller school divisions or private schools may look at this specialty area and decide that it is best to contract out the work. This may not save money. Still, it is perhaps superior to in-house hiring, since employees with these skills often go from job to job to the highest bidder. It is difficult for a smaller division to have the funds to be competitive for the personnel. Therefore, contracting the work to an outside organization may make sense. Larger school districts will need a division within their facility departments to work with telecommunications and information technologies, or this portion of facilities management may be integrated into the operation of the technology department. Whatever way it is organized, the two departments will need to work closely together.

One of the most critical times of cooperation is when a new facility is being planned and constructed. Designing the specifications, deciding where the drops for the phones and computers will be, determining how many drops need to be installed, and trying to make a decision on whether or not to go wireless are just a few decisions to be made. This is one instance in building management where a consultant should be hired who is knowledgeable about school facilities, school telecommunication and technology needs, and who comes highly recommended by other school divisions and high-tech vendors. Although the architect may have someone employed who is an expert in the field, it is important to get more than one opinion. Trying to make uninformed decisions in this area nearly always leads to a costlier installation.

Web-Enabled Facility Management and Maintenance

Facility managers now have the tools to be as responsive to their clients as could be imagined just a few years ago. With the opportunity to web-base either through a school system Internet or intranet, the maintenance department can be as close as the computer. Web-enabled systems provide on-line access for customers, other agencies, and the public, where necessary. They also allow the maintenance department to control and manage loads, schedules and information and to integrate information more efficiently. They permit centralized information control and access. Perhaps one of the most important points to be made is that a Web-based system permits the maintenance department to use technology that is already a part of the school district's infrastructure.

The software used to initiate such a system, whether off-the-shelf or custom-designed, should be able to be integrated or coupled into the energy management system, CMMS, or any of the other systems discussed in this chapter. To optimize the use of a technology system for the maintenance and engineering department, it is imperative that all programs are compatible and work together.

Web-based programs can assist in greater efficiency and improve the bottom line, while making the operation more attuned to the needs of the occupants of the facility.

Evaluating the Cost Savings That Might Result from Outsourcing of Technology Systems and Staff

Outsourcing may or may not produce a savings. Outsourcing may be as simple as contracting someone to produce a product for the maintenance department or it may be as complicated as letting a request for proposal for the management of a portion or all of a department.

Inefficiencies can hurt the bottom line of any spreadsheet. Often personnel in maintenance departments are not inept, but they are short handed, are responsible for too many tasks, and are not specialized enough to conduct the work. This leads to work that may not be satisfactory for the customer. This may be a time when a service is outsourced. While the district's employees are focusing on the core work, the technology management company can be attending to the portion of the department that has been neglected. Here is an example. Four years ago in a mid-size school district on the East Coast, the employees were about to mutiny because the computers and networks were not being maintained. The organization was fortunate to have a lot of hardware and software, but it worked inefficiently, repairs were sluggish, and the network was always down. By the time one problem was fixed, two more were reported. If a new, capable employee was hired, one that knew the technology system, they soon were hired by industry for a higher salary.

A task force brainstormed the problems and decided that the maintenance of the computer equipment, the operation of the network including web accessibility and e-mail, and the development and maintenance of the databases were just too much for the school district to maintain and supervise. This does not even begin to consider the repairs of all of the related hardware and corresponding systems. The task force decided to develop a request for proposal (RFP) to outsource the technology department.

There were two responses to the RFP; one was accepted, and a contract was negotiated. The company that won the contract conducted an extensive feasibility study, so that the needs of the school district were fully covered in the proposed contract. The contract included personnel to manage the overall operation, do computer repairs, and oversee installations. This freed up the other technology employees to have time to maintain the network, databases, and system software. The company awarded the contract was responsible for hiring their personnel and for providing their remuneration. This was another task that was removed from the technology department.

This instance of outsourcing:

(1) allowed the organization/school district employees to focus on the core business;

(2) eliminated work overlay and, thus, enabled the school district to reduce FTE costs-or to free the time for the employees to get their jobs done more efficiently, proving greater customer satisfaction;

(3) provided one point of accountability for computer repair (this decreased "finger pointing" dramatically);

(4) offered a solution so that the repair contract hired employees with the skills necessary to do the job well and provided regular retraining;

(5) and improved workflow and productivity.

Therefore, in this example, costs were lowered, there was a higher quality of service, and customer satisfaction improved. Turnover became less of a problem, as employees were happier, and the contracting company was able to offer more competitive salaries.

One might say: "How can money be saved, if the salaries of the repair personnel are competitive?" This may be the portion of the contract where the costs that are passed on to the school organization are not lower. However, school division employee morale is not as negatively affected by the higher salaries being paid by the outsourcer, as they would be if the school district were paying them. The savings come with efficiency, having the most skilled workers possible, and releasing the school district employees to get their jobs done without the interruption of hardware problems.

Reference

Coggan, D. A. (1999, July). Building automation made simple. Retrieved July 14, 2002, from http://www.automatedbuildings.com/news/jul99/articles/coggan/coggan.htm.

CHAPTER 9

Contract Maintenance—External Management Service

S CHOOL systems across the nation are attempting to satisfy a public mission that is an inherent dilemma: operate on less funding, which will keep taxes low, and continue to improve services. The private school's dilemma is not unlike the public school's: keep tuition low, yet provide an inviting, safe facility and improve services. Privatization, outsourcing, and contracted services, are ways localities and private educational organizations are trying to meet conflicting demands.

Description of Services

School organizations, both public and private across the nation, are turning to outside services, which from solely managerial services of custodial and grounds or maintenance to copier repair, mechanical, energy management services, and computer repair and software maintenance. (Food service and transportation are other areas that are contracted out; however, these will not be discussed.) Contracted maintenance is the transferring of tasks previously performed by the educational organization's personnel to private, for-profit businesses and industries.

External contract maintenance groups simply manage the local organization's personnel and provide certain materials and supplies. Internal maintenance services bring their own personnel into the organization. Whatever the extent of the services, materials, and supplies that are a part of the contracted services, the local organization should have a predetermined administrative oversight process to assure that the public or private school is being served to the contract.

The reputations of companies that regularly provide contracted services have been tarnished during past years, as it is not an easy task to convert from work being done by the local organization to having an "outsider" come into the schools and begin to make changes. Organizational change is never easy, and inviting outsiders to play a role in change opens the door to apprehension and perceived threats. This chapter discusses the advantages, as well as disadvantages, of having an outside contractor.

There are several organizational models for school maintenance and operations that may be outsourced, or any one or a combination may be used:

(1) An organization may keep all district or private school personnel, but outsource the management of the operation.

(2) An internal organizational manager and employees perform all in-house maintenance, operations, and grounds functions, except emergency work, specialized trades and crafts, small and specialized projects, and any complex, personnel-intensive work, which are contracted to outside sources.

(3) An organization uses many in-house employees, but organizes major positions of each venue to be contracted to outside vendors to maximize the time of organizational personnel.

(4) All but the supervisors are employees of the vendor.

Who Provides Such Services?

If the educational organization, either public or private, has a task or service that it wishes to have conducted by an outside firm, all that needs to be done is to put a request for proposal (RFP) on the street, and companies will respond. Be assured, however, that issuing an RFP will create a stressful situation for employees concerned about their working conditions, benefits, pay, and ultimately, their jobs. Whatever the content of the RFP, the locality or private educational organization needs to make very sure that all outside vendors have equal opportunities to be considered for the proposal process.

Recommendations of specific vendors cannot be made here. Performance criteria exist that should be considered by the school district or private educational organizations when considering a decision to outsource any functions of operations and facility management.

Initially the educational organization should assess the total operation and performance of the maintenance function that is being accomplished in house. Some of these work activities are noted in Figure 9.1. This list is not conclusive, but it will assist in familiarizing the administrator with the various responsibilities that should be considered prior to any RFPs being let. A grading system should be used to evaluate the functions.

Support Area	Performance Criteria/Activities
Custodial	• Cost per student for labor • Cost per student for materials, supplies, and annually for equipment • Average square feet maintained per custodian • Quality of service delivered or desired • Staff development for supervisors and employees • Overall cost of service delivered • Cost of supervision per student and custodian
Maintenance (Including HVAC)	• Cost per student for labor • Cost annually for equipment, supplies, and materials per student • Effectiveness of preventive maintenance • Quality of service delivered or desired • Staff Development for supervisors and employees • Overall cost of service delivered • Cost of supervision per student and maintenance worker
Grounds	• Cost per student per acre of land for labor • Cost of supervision per student and per grounds keeper • Cost annually for equipment, supplies, and materials per student • Overall cost of service delivered

Figure 9-1 Possible Facilities Support Performance Criteria and Activities.

Once these data are available for the in-house operation, the school system or private organization will be in a position to assess the pros and cons of maintaining the current division of labor, or seeking to outsource the services.

After these data are assessed, the business department, working with the legal consultant and the maintenance and operations leadership, is ready to solicit proposals from vendors. A well-planned process should be in place to select the proposals that best meet the requirements of the RFP. This planning will provide assurance for current employees, allow the stakeholders to participate, and ensure that the best proposal is selected. Once the best proposal is selected, the business department should negotiate with the vendor. This negotiation is the pivot for the success of outsourcing.

At this point, the school organization becomes a purchaser of services, and competition in the business sector is used manipulatively to provide the safest, most efficient services for the least cost. Therefore, the negotiator not only needs to be cognizant of the school's operational needs, but also be a knowledgeable and aggressive negotiator. The maintenance director should be involved, as well. This will make the process less intimidating for employees, since someone with whom they are familiar is part of the process for change and is representing their interests.

Negotiating the contract requires professional oversight. Not only does the scope of the work need to be carefully delineated, there should be specific language as to what services are to be provided, at what times the work should be performed, and how schedules will be established. Clear definitions must be worked out for what an emergency is, what extenuating circumstances are, and how normal operations are defined. No detail is too small for discussion, and any critical detail needs to be a part of the contract. Critical to the success of the contract negotiations is being able to trust the parties who are at the table. This needs to be an open process, with both parties negotiating with integrity and openness. The length of the contract is critical. It is important not to be locked into a

Category	Examples
Maintenance	• HVAC (including energy management, installations, and repair) • Security systems • Elevator service, repair, and certification • Safety systems such as sprinkler systems, fire extinguishers, and fire alarms • Kitchen and refrigeration equipment • Staff development (including safety training) • Technology equipment repair
Construction/Renovation	• General contracting • Sidewalk replacement, repairs, and other concrete work • Installing portable classrooms, ramps, and decks • Flooring and lighting installations and lowering ceilings • Roof maintenance, repairs, and installations • Painting
Grounds	• Mowing, weeding, edging, and other landscaping services • Athletic field upkeep and preparation • Bleacher and playground repairs • Paving, painting, lighting, and other parking lot maintenance • Irrigation and other watering systems • Fencing installation and repairs
Custodial	• Janitorial services • Staff development (including safety training and preparing personnel for certain licensure)
Other Services	• Pest control (indoor and outside) • Water and/or sewer treatment or repairs to equipment and other specialized testing services • Engineering services • Surveying, architectural, and/or legal services

Figure 9-2 Examples of Activities That Can Be Contracted to an Outside Organization.

long-term contract. Also, legal review will disclose the ramifications of a maintenance contract for other contracts. A good contract will always allow for as much flexibility in timing and handling of personnel as possible, especially if labor issues are involved.

When the best contract has been negotiated, the appropriate administrator presents the contract to the superintendent and board. The processes are different, based on the locality or whether or not the organization is public or private. This is another point of the process when employees must be at the table, so they will hear the information from management and not from external sources. In addition, the plan and contract taken to the school board need to include an implementation process. Although board approval is considered the culminating activity by most employees, unless personnel are involved and made aware of what is going on, board approval may be the beginning of the end. Employees can make or break initiatives in contract maintenance or external management services.

Outside services may be sought for any of the following reasons; however, the list is not complete nor should it confine the educational organization to only the areas suggested in Figure 9-2.

Pros and Cons

The pros and cons of contract maintenance or contracting out maintenance services are very similar. Any differences will be noted throughout the discussion.

Pros

The following are advantages of outsourcing. School organizations should keep in mind that the resources and needs of the locality or the private school organization should be the driving force in a decision on whether or not to use contract maintenance or to contract any of the maintenance operations. It is not simply a decision based on money.

(1) By responding to the demands of the citizenry and governing bodies for more efficient, lower-cost external services, the organization's employees may become more efficient and innovative. Thus, there is a cost saving from simply the suggestion of outsourcing.

(2) Government bodies generally are not encouraged to be competitive with the services they provide; contracting services and operations implicitly endorses enterprise and competition.

(3) Any savings from outsourcing can be redirected to neglected services or maintenance, to the instructional program, or to lower taxes.

(4) Contracting out is a method to provide services when there is a shortage of available laborers and/or the in-house staff has limited ability. In addition, specialized tasks may be outsourced on an "as-needed" basis.

(5) The most up-to-date facilities management training and materials and services can be made a part of the contract. Local governing bodies will accept this through a contracted service; however, they either could not or would not provide the same line items in the budget if they were obligated to fund the staff development or materials. Local governing bodies by law are required to accept the least expensive bid.

(6) The ultimate goal generally is to save management time and to reduce operating costs. This must be done while improving the quality of the maintenance and operational functions. According to a report prepared by the Association of School Business Officials International (ASBO), most maintenance employees are only between 25 to 35 percent productive due to poor management techniques. In 1997, the International Facilities Management Association noted nearly $1.00 per square foot savings on outsourced contracts.

(7) Private schools can become more competitive in recruiting and keeping students, if they have a well-maintained facility. This is also an advantage for public schools.

Cons

The first question is: if an educational operation has an efficient, effective, and competent operation and workforce, why would it be an advantage to outsource by not only paying for the service but also underwriting a company's profit? In addition, simply the hint that services are going to be outsourced causes morale problems within the ranks of the employees, who become concerned about their jobs, who is going to supervise them, and what other impacts such a move might make on their job security and day-to-day operations. Other questions of importance are concerns about contract oversight for the required services, who decides if the contract is being adhered to, and how the contractor will affect instructional functions. Inefficient oversight may lead to an inadequate contract. It is important to know, too, how the contracted services and personnel will interface with existing maintenance operations or other support functions and staff.

Costs and Possible Savings through Contracting-Out Maintenance and Operations

Managers first determine the scope of work being contracted and its related cost. The first drives the second. Time needs to be allotted to develop a scope of work that articulates the labor, materials, and other cost issues.

The best way to consider costs of outsourcing may be to consider an actual RFP process and how potential cost is computed. An illustration follows of how education management services were actually contracted, between a large corporation and a local school board.

In the early 1990s, it was evident that the custodial grounds department of the school division was inferior. The leadership did not possess the appropriate skills to lead a department of such magnitude, equipment was of poor quality or non-existent, and employees had not been trained. The school board appointed a local committee to work on improving the condition of facilities and the outside appearance. It was decided to let a request for proposal to see if a management firm would be interested in supplying such services. Immediately, employees were concerned, as they were afraid they would lose their jobs, and did not realize that the local school authority was dedicated to the concept that no jobs would be eliminated, except those that were affected by attrition. A series of meetings were held to keep employees abreast of pertinent information about the contract process.

The local school division retained the large corporation (from this point to be called ABC) to provide management services of the custodial and grounds employees. ABC agreed to manage and direct all employees, and to provide all necessary training equipment, films, slides, literature, daily work and project schedules, indices, standard operational procedures, and training manuals. ABC also contracted to provide all coordinating management personnel, which in its judgment were necessary to properly perform the management services. These decisions were not made without ABC making an initial on-site visit, which included interviews with administrators, teachers, principals, and custodians. They evaluated equipment, supplies, cleaning schedules, and quality (See Figure 9.1).

During the initial visit, ABC found that staff was highly motivated but in need of the following:

- Training
- Supervision
- Quality standards
- A management system
- Cleaner schools
- Balanced schedules
- Regulatory compliance
- Cost effectiveness

The management system included putting into place standardized chemicals, equipment, training, quality assurances, and higher expectations of performance for support staff.

After the first year of the contract with ABC, interviews with personnel noted improved quality of services, improved employee morale and skills, and a wiser use of resources. For the first time, employees had the training necessary to do a competent job, as well as the equipment and supplies to make that possible. When administrators or school board members interviewed the workers, they discovered a new pride in the services they were providing. This contract was so successful that a few years later ABC was contracted for copier and audiovisual machine repair service. Three years after that contract was initiated, the same type of contract was arranged for computer repair.

Besides potential cost savings, there are advantages to an outside contract:

(1) School administrators' time is saved for other tasks.

(2) Experts in the field can be called in to perform duties.

(3) Often, schools that had previously performed their duties with inadequate equipment and had a funding body that would not provide for necessary materials and supplies can get these included in a management contract.

(4) Quality control can be addressed to one individual in charge of the contracted services.

In 2000, a supplement published to School Business Affairs (ASBO, 2000) noted regional maintenance and operations costs in dollars per student and square foot during the 1999-2000 school year. A copy of these costs can be used,

States	Cost Per Student	Cost Per Square Foot
CT, MA, ME, NJ, RI, VT	$622.48	$3.87
NJ, NY	$692.57	$5.28
DC, DE, MD,PA, VA, WV	$617.89	$4.19
AL FL, GA, KY, MS, NC, SC, TN	$489.84	$3.02
IL, IN, MI, MN, OH, WI	$627.88	$4.03
AR, LA, MN, OK, TX	$572.29	$2.96
IA, KS, MO, NE	$524.60	$3.28
CO, MT, ND, SD, UT, WY	$480.80	$3.14
AZ, CA, HI, NV	$537.59	$5.39
AK, ID, OR, WA	$632.55	$4.92

Figure 9-3 Maintenance and Operations Costs, Per Student and Square Foot.

plus an inflationary rates to project what a school organizations costs may be and to compare costs proposed by a management company.

Contract Development

Developing the contract cannot be rushed. The contract is the guide by which the school division and contractor must abide for the term of the agreement. Taking time at the beginning will save time, money, and stress later. Private schools and public educational organizations should use their lawyers, review other schools' contracts, and become very familiar with the agreement before recommending that the superintendent or board chairperson sign it. When it is time for the contract to be renewed, once more there should be a thorough review.

References

Maintenance & operations solutions: Meeting the challenge of improving school facilities. *School Business Affairs* (supplement). (2000). Reston, VA: ASBO International.Using Student Input: Achievement and Opinion

Note: The authors would like to thank Gloucester County Public Schools, Gloucester, Virginia, for the specific contract information in this chapter. They have had successful management and technology contracts for several years and would be an excellent contact.

CHAPTER 10

Regulatory Aspects of Maintenance and Operations

Water Quality and Testing

A school's water supply must be safe, and the state has an interest in monitoring water purity. Every school administrator who has had a water test come back contaminated, knows the safety concerns and the challenges of dealing with parents and employees, while trying to correct the problem. In a specific case, the level of lead in a school's drinking water exceeded the safety guidelines. Parents were very cooperative while the source of the lead was tracked down. However, the bottled water dispensers had not been removed from the same school, when harmful bacteria were found in the same school's drinking water. Parents were not as understanding with the second problem. It became difficult for the school cafeteria to operate using bottled water. Every parent and school community has the right to know and to be confident that a school's water is safe.

Regulatory Agencies

Every state has its own set of agencies that monitor drinking water, especially well water. Agencies include: departments of agriculture, consumer services, soil and water conservation, recreation, planning, cooperative extension, environmental quality water division, environmental quality waste division, and many others. The departments of health, housing, marine resources, and even the department of transportation may have policies or regulations that affect the local school maintenance department.

It is not always easy to deal with these regulatory organizations. Just to learn their vocabulary is a challenge. However, most of the agencies are willing to work with the school district or private schools. One person should be appointed as the contact and the maintenance employee responsible for adherence to regulations. Schools with well water should have trained operators for their water-works and wastewater. Some states require licensure for this position and have classes of expertise.

Cross-Connection Control

Cross-connections are the links through which it is possible for contamination to enter a potable water supply. Contaminants enter the water system when the pressure of the polluted source exceeds the pressure of the potable source. Public health officials have long been concerned with such pollution, as history shows that water supply contamination has resulted from cross-connections. As early as 1933 in Chicago, such contamination resulted in 1,409 persons contracting amebic dysentery. This and other epidemics resulted from contamination introduced into a water supply through improper plumbing. Thus, public health officials have implemented policies and regulations to control drinking water, and school officials need to have trained personnel to make sure that students and staff have a safe potable supply. School staff plumbers must know that hydraulic and pollution factors may combine to produce a sanitary hazard. They must know reliable and simple standards for backflow prevention, and all maintenance employees should be made aware that the hazards resulting from direct connections greatly outweigh the convenience gained.

Administration of regulations

Most states provide waterworks regulations to school organizations. These regulations include procedures, emergency information, enforcement guidelines, and exemptions or variances, and a complete plan for monitoring, record keeping, and reporting. The manual will note all standards, operational information, and design issues. Every maintenance department should have copies of such regulations and policies and also have one maintenance worker responsible for making sure that the regulations are enforced. This includes monitoring frequency, being familiar organic and inorganic compounds, knowing where samples should be taken, and having a personality that is effective and does not generate undue alarm. All analyses ought to be performed in accordance with the regulatory guidelines, and the laboratories used for testing must have the necessary certification of the state agency in charge of waterworks management.

Notifying public

Should any contaminants or problems be found with the water system, most states have very stringent rules as to how the public is to be notified. These should be followed in detail. Even if the public is not required to be notified of certain problems, it often behooves the administrator to do so, in order to squelch rumors.

Air Quality, Radon

How many of us know very much about the air we breathe? According to Facilitymanagement.com, both residential and commercial facilities may have more air pollution than some of the major industrial cities. Since we spend approximately 90 percent of our time indoors, risks from indoor air pollution are increased. The literature also indicates that the young are very susceptible to indoor pollutants.

Causes of Poor Indoor Air Quality

Causes of poor indoor air range from faulty ventilation systems to buildings that were not designed for the number of students and employees housed in the facility. Carpet, pressed wood, cleaning materials, copy machine fumes, restroom air fresheners, adhesives, and many other sources produce indoor air pollutants. Ventilation systems may have accumulated dirt and other contaminants over the years. Water-damaged walls and carpets from flooding or a condenser overflow can be a breeding ground for mold and mildew. These systems can also be a breeding ground for biological contaminants, which are introduced into the building air from cooling towers, air conditioners, humidifiers, and other ventilation equipment *(Facility Management.com)*.

There have been times over the years that certain buildings seem to be the cause of illness, but the direct relationship could not be pinpointed. Sneezing, watery eyes, rashes, runny noises, and other discomforts may be the symptoms. Some may complain of irritability or lethargy, upset stomach, and headaches. The symptoms are numerous, and the cause is elusive. If there is a relationship between the complaints and the building, the building may be labeled a "sick" building, and a monumental effort may be expended to find the causes.

Often a facility was designed for one purpose, but used for another. This happens more frequently in our schools that we like to admit; however, funds are always scarce, so support personnel try to make the best use of the floor space they have. This may mean that a computer laboratory is installed in what was formerly a room expected to have low occupancy. Ventilation for that space was not designed for 20 students, a teacher, 20 computers, and printers.

Building facilities are more airtight. Synthetic building materials are utilized, and people are more ardent about housekeeping supplies and the use of pesticides. Combined with the concern about economy with ventilation systems, the delay of maintenance to save money, and HVAC systems that are undersized, we tend to create air quality problems for ourselves.

Health Effects

Some of the health effects were mentioned in the above section, but they are by no means the only symptoms. They maladies range from asthma, Legionnaire's disease, to certain types of pneumonia, or psychological stress and discomfort. According to the World Health Organization, as high as 30 percent of renovated or new facilities generate air quality complaints from the occupants. This is of great concern when one considers that one in five Americans spend their days in elementary and secondary schools. In addition, a 1995 study of the General Accounting Office reported approximately 50 percent of our schools have indoor air quality problems.

Facilitymanagemnt.com noted that poor indoor air quality can have many negative health effects on students and employees:

(1) There is an increased incidence of long- and short-term health problems.
(2) A reduced comfort, attendance rate, and productivity are noted.
(3) There is a tendency for faster deterioration and reduced efficiency of the facility and the related equipment.
(4) Increased workers' compensation claims are on record.

Conducting a Building Inspection

Whether there appears to be an air quality problem or not, periodic building investigations should be conducted. These investigations may be in the form of questionnaires that are distributed to the facility users, or the support personnel may personally conduct reviews on site.

If there are problems, it is not unlikely that there will be a need for interviews at the site and inspections of ventilation systems, HVAC controls, and a review of building features that may cause problems. If there are indications of moisture problems or chemical sources to air pollution, a consultant may need to be hired to identify problem sources, as well as the pollutants in the air.

A consultant or review may tell you more than you really want to know as a person responsible for the facility. However, such knowledge may be necessary to protect the welfare and safety of students and employees. One author faced a problem first hand, when the governing body refused to move school offices from what appeared to be a building plagued by various molds and mildews. Employees had numerous health problems related to respiratory illnesses, but there was no clear evidence that the building in which they worked was the culprit. After a scientific consultant was hired, and the various molds were identified, the governing body was more agreeable to vacating the facility.

Radon

According to the Environmental Protection Agency (EPA), radon comes from the natural breakdown of uranium in soil, rock, and water, and gets into the air. It moves up through the ground through cracks and other holes in a foundation. Buildings trap it inside, where the gas can build up. Testing is the only way to know whether or not indoor air contains this radioactive gas. After smoking, it is the second leading cause of lung cancer in the United States.

According to the EPA, the amount of radon in the air is measured in "picoCuries (pCi/L) per liter of air." (Some scientists use Working Levels rather than picoCuries.) School support employees should contact the State radon office for a list of testers. The tester should be certified to conduct such testing. High levels of radon have been found in schools across the country. The EPA conducted a survey that estimates that nearly one in five schools has at least one school room with a short-term radon level above the action level of 4 pCi/L-the level at which it is recommended that schools take action.

Testing is relatively inexpensive and should definitely be conducted in classrooms that are at or below ground level. Testing should be done during the cooler months of the year-months that school is generally in session—and when windows can be kept closed for the testing.

What Will It Cost If Radon Is in Our School?

The testing is relatively inexpensive. Testing kits (EPA approved) are available commercially, or the school system can hire a certified contractor to do the work. If the testing results are higher than the recommended standards and the school fails its radon test, there are proven techniques available that will lower radon levels and the risks of lung disease from exposure. The solution may entail a change in the ventilation system, although that may cause a loss of efficiency, which will increase utility bills. It may be as simple as fixing cracks in the foundation or cement flooring. However, the EPA (1992) recommends using a contractor when fixing radon problems. To hire such a contractor, the agency recommends working with the following checklist (this checklist should be used whether hiring a professional with or without a bidding process, Figure 10-1):

As with other products, school officials need to look not only at current costs, but also at the cost to maintain the proposed system. The initial cost, however, is difficult to estimate, as it will vary according to the complexity of the problem.

Radon Reduction Processes

The contractor that is hired should conduct a visual inspection of the facilities. From that inspection, a system should be designed that considers the features of the building, as well as the severity of the radon problem. This is where the contractor may recommend diagnostic tests to assist with finding the best deterrent to the gas. This may include soil suctions, ventilation of crawl spaces, sealing surfaces that are ground level, pressurization at the lower levels of the facility, and ventilation of living areas. There should be a warning device placed where it can be seen or heard easily by school administrators that shows when the system is not working properly. This is utmost importance for a safe and healthy radon

YES	NO	Questions to Ask Contractors
		Will the contractor provide references or photographs, as well as test results of 'before' and 'after' radon levels of past radon reduction work?
		Can the contractor explain what the work will involve, how long it will take to complete, and exactly how the radon reduction system will work?
		Does the contractor charge a fee for any diagnostic tests? Although many contractors give free estimates, they may charge for diagnostic tests-these tests help determine what radon reduction system should be used, but are not always necessary
		Will the contractor inspect your building structure before giving you an estimate?
		Will the contractor show a proof of liability insurance, bonding, and licensure?
		Will the contractor provide you with a guarantee to reduce the radon levels to 4 pCi/L or below, and if so, for how long?
		Will the contactor review the quality of your radon measurement results and determine if EPA testing procedures were followed?

Figure 10-1 Checklist for Evaluating Contractors.

reduction system, as well as to assure that there are not problems that develop in a building that has tested negative. Finally, if a school has its own well water, it, too, should be tested for radon.

For All Air Quality Concerns

There are many indoor air quality (IAQ) concerns: asbestos, radon, airborne mold and mildew, personal hygiene products and other odors, pesticides, poor ventilation, noxious chemicals, cleaning agents, too much or too little humidity, improperly maintained air filters, dust, and many more. They must investigate, be proactive, and take each complaint as a possible indication of an existing problem.

Asbestos

Prior to 1986, asbestos was used in many building materials, because it was strong, fire resistant, and a very good insulator, although it was first noted as a possible health hazard in the 1920s after asbestosis became recognized (Fumento, 1990). Many schools installed flooring materials, pipes with insulation, and ceiling tiles that contained asbestos. Then it was discovered that asbestos fibers were causing health problems, especially with employees who worked in positions where the fibers became airborne (friable asbestos), increasing the likelihood that the fibers would be inhaled. On October 22, 1986, the Asbestos Hazard Emergency Response Act (AHERA) was signed into law. It provided guidelines to manage asbestos-containing materials in schools.

AHERA requires school organizations to have a designated, trained coordinator. The AHERA-designated person is responsible for the following:

(1) Identifying friable (readily crumbled by hand) and non-friable (fibers that are not likely to be airborne unless disturbed) asbestos materials;

(2) Developing an asbestos management plan, which is available to faculty, staff, parents, or other interested parties for each facility;

(3) Implementing the programs for managing the facilities, which have asbestos materials, especially those containing asbestos materials needing abatement;

(4) Conducting semi-annual reviews of the surveillance and management activities, including taking appropriate response actions and maintaining adequate records;

(5) Notifying annually all staff and students' parents or guardians concerning the status of asbestos-containing materials.

The risk to students and employees is believed by some experts to be minimal. Hans Weill, M.D. and Janet M. Hughes of Tulane University put the annual risk figure for school exposure at approximately 0.25 deaths per million exposed (Fumento, 1990). However, the Environmental Protection Agency (EPA) requires every school in the United States, regardless of the date of construction, to maintain a management plan. If an inspection confirms that no friable or non-friable asbestos materials are contained in the facility, then inspections processes can be terminated. If a new school or other school facility is built, the architect or a certified building inspector can sign a statement of exclusion of asbestos-containing materials. This statement is then submitted to the EPA, for the facility to be removed from the list of schools requiring inspections.

The facilities director, central office staff, and the school board should endeavor to provide custodial and maintenance employees with the appropriate training, as long as any facilities contain asbestos, and there is a management plan in effect. The staff development should be done annually, as well as training for new employees during the year. The latter is particularly important—

training for new employees or outside contractors who may be working in a school facility with non-friable asbestos. During a renovation of an older school, a contractor was told explicitly not to disturb certain floor tiles. The teachers in the building were very aware of the asbestos-containing floor tiles and reported early one school day that their tile was being removed. When the administration learned of the disturbance of the asbestos-containing floor tile, the school had to be closed and all contracting ceased, while a licensed company was hired to abate all remaining asbestos, conduct a thorough cleaning, and log numerous tests to assure teachers, parents, and the public that the facility was safe to use. Lack of communication or training regarding asbestos can lead to disruption.

Americans with Disabilities Act Regulations (ADA)

The 101st Congress enacted the Americans with Disabilities Act in 1990 to establish a concise and comprehensive law to prohibit discrimination on the basis of disability. No other department within the school system was impacted by this act as much as facilities operations. From floor and sidewalk surfaces, restrooms, signage, parking spaces, to stairs, handrails, grab bars, and entrances, nearly every structure within the school district has a component covered by the ADA. In addition, facilities departments had to consider accessibility for students and employees, as well as the community. Classrooms were required to be accessible, as well as the personnel office for job applicants. Students require access to all programs. Parents or guardians must have access to all activities that involve their children. It is important that students are aware of the importance of adhering to the ADA.

When the law became effective, school districts across the nation were concerned that the act was so strict that it would be impossible to implement all aspects of the code. However, even though it is taking years in some instances to adhere to all of the compliance issues of the ADA, the government has seemed to take a "common sense" approach to enforcement. Enforcement has been based on "reasonable accommodation" and fairness. This is interpreted by school personnel to mean that all programs are accessible to students and staff, not necessarily all facilities. As money becomes available, and renovations and new facilities are brought on line, all tenets of the law should be implemented. The government has cooperated with school districts in their implementation processes, as long as it is obvious that there is intent to adhere to the law and an expedient plan is in place to accomplish this.

ADA compliance raises cost concerns. However, many times an access challenge can be met with appropriate reasonable accommodation at little or no cost, if all aspects of the problem are studied. Sears conducted a study of 436 reasonable accommodations that its company provided over a fourteen-year period. Of those, 69 percent cost nothing, 28 percent cost less than $1,000, and only 3 percent cost more than $1,000 (USDOJ.gov). Although it is always easier to adhere to ADA when building a new facility, alternative costs may be controlled by installing ramps, lowering work tables, rearranging desks and other furniture, removing one bathroom stall wall, changing the room where the activity occurs, or adding handicap accessible attachments for door knobs.

There may be instances when all manner of thought is given to a situation, but it will cost the school district considerable money to provide access. For instance, a doorway is not wide enough to provide wheelchair access. Even though the hinges are recessed, the doorway is still too narrow. The only recourse is to widen the opening. Or there may be a situation when a ramp is not feasible, and a lift or elevator must be installed. It is in such situations that the school district must budget and make the accommodation within a reasonable time.

It is sometimes overlooked that Title II of the ADA addresses employment practices of state and local governments. In 1992 Title II became effective to prohibit discrimination against qualified individuals with disabilities. This includes job application procedures, hiring, firing, promotion, compensation, and any other employment terms, regulations, and provisions. The phrase "qualified individual with a disability" is taken directly from the ADA and includes any person who meets the legitimate skill requirements, experience, education, or any other requirements of an employment position that he or she holds or seeks and who can perform the "essential functions" (another ADA phrase) of the position with or without reasonable accommodation (ADA). The facilities department must work with the department of human resources to assure that this provision of the law is followed, when recruiting and hiring personnel.

What Are the Costs of Complying with Federal Regulations?

Often when a regulation is first put into effect, those not supporting it cite cost as an impediment. Asbestos abatement may be one of the most expensive regulatory mandates. This is due to several reasons, including scientific testing and the fact that licensed personnel and firms must be used to remove the material, and disposal is also an expensive component. Asbestos abatement in a single facility can easily cost the school organization thousands of dollars. In the areas of scientific testing of air, water, and other components of our environment, cost should not be a factor that inhibits implementation. There are certain regulations that must be adhered to -to the letter of the law-as they were put in place for the safety of the inhabitants of the facility. The only cost cutting may be bidding the testing to the lowest bidder, but the work must be done for the safety and security of all involved.

References

Asbestos HazardousEmergency Response Act (AHERA). 1986 (P.L. 99-519), Amended 1990 (P.L. 101-637).

Employment. Retrieved May 1, 2002, from http://www.istal.com/smoke/ADA Handbook/ADA FAX.text.

Fumento, M. (1990, January). The asbestos rip-off. *Reader's Digest* [On-line]. Retrieved May 2, 2002, from http://www.fumento.com/asbest2.html.

Indoor air quality concerns. Facility managemnt.com [On-line]. Retrieved April 16, 2002, from http://www.facilitymanagemnt.com/articles/artiq.html.

Myths and facts about the Americans with Disabilities Act. Retrieved April 24, 2002, from http://www.usdoj.gov/crt/ada/pubs/mythfct.txt.

United States Environmental Protection Agency. (1992, August). *Consumer's guide to radon reduction.* (Office of Air and Radiation [6609J]).

CHAPTER 11

Cost-Effective Procurement Processes

CONSIDER general procurement costs as noted in Figure 11-1. They are not negligible and they run the gamut.

The above are just a few of the considerations to be made during the procurement process and provides a short list of items that add to the cost of the product or service.

Before any process begins, there are likely to be local and state procurement manuals that need to be read. No amount of negotiations, or astute purchasing, can substitute for the regulations of procurement. It may be, if there is a complicated or very large purchase to be made, that the school district legal counsel needs to be consulted. In some school organizations this is not an option, but a requirement.

Once the rules and regulations are fully known, there are several procedures to follow:

(1) Develop a set of specifications. Be sure to work with the experts and technicians to assure that the correct specifications are written. Again, money saved upfront will be wiped out if the incorrect product is purchased or if equipment is purchased that will not stand long-term wear and tear.

(2) Work with vendors to get the best price for the quantity that is needed for the school district.

(3) Make sure that the place of delivery and the amount of handling do not cause the cost to be increased. Materials that must be loaded and unloaded multiple times may be more expensive in the long run, once you calculate the labor costs. In the same vein, if a warehouse must be heated to keep a product from freezing, it may be less expensive to pay extra transportation costs to have the materials delivered to the end-user's site.

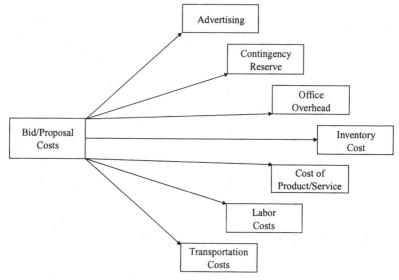

Figure 11-1 Cost of Procurement.

(4) Add sufficient shipping costs to assure a speedy delivery; this may cost less than having one of your schools or departments run out of supplies.

(5) Work to assure that billing costs are kept to a minimum. Automation of the process will save labor costs, as well as handling errors.

(6) Arrange for on-site training and assure that all manuals are delivered to the job site, with someone in charge of filing them in a safe place;

(7) Choosing nearby suppliers at a slightly higher cost may save an equal or greater amount in shipping.

(8) Even though the locality may have rules and regulations that pressure the school system to accept the lowest price, be willing to contest such a purchase if the product or service is known to be inferior. There is generally a procedure for such a process. Be willing to fight for durability, dependability, service, and safety.

(9) Take advantage of any economies of scale.

Those in charge of procurement may find other ways to save, such as making a purchase during the off-season or by advance ordering. Smart purchasers also consult others in the school organization who have made such purchases previously.

During every portion of every step of this process, make sure that counsel is kept informed. Legal counsel should protect the school through contract terms, limitations on delivery schedules, or clauses for contract breach. Counsel must protect the interests of the school organization to assure that vendors do not take advantage of the maintenance department. Counsel especially needs to be a part of large contracts, such as those negotiated with architects, roofers, or management companies. Large professional firms or vending contractors will have their lawyers writing and developing their contracts, so the interests of the school organization must be protected. Negotiating the contract without counsel in such instances will usually prove to be shortsighted.

CHAPTER 12

Deciding to Renovate

Value of Renovating

A school building is a community asset. Even buildings that are considered old are viewed as assets because of the investment a community has made in them over the years. In many instances, an older building is of great importance because of its location. The building may have historical value, special architectural features, or interior space that can be used for a variety of purposes by the school system and community. Even if the school population is removed from a building, there is value in the structure to the community. As an asset, the building needs to be properly maintained and preserved. Renovating an existing structure is one way to preserve building value-both for a school district and the larger community.

The intrinsic replacement value of a school building might be much higher than the actual dollar value of replacement because of the community interests in this asset. Many community members, whether parents or not, feel the school is the heart of the community. It is a central point of attention for all neighborhood members, and it is often in a location, such as near a park or center, where non-education-related functions important to the community. This is often true for private and parochial school buildings. A parochial or private school building is regarded as the heart of an extended community, no matter where the students may live.

The practical value of the educational structure and in many cases the emotional ties parents and community members have for the building, can make renovation an attractive alternative to constructing a new facility. Even when the school building is not used by community members for any purpose other than schooling, there can be a great deal of sentiment regarding the school structure because it represents or stands for the community, especially if the building is named for the community in which it is located.

There are many reasons for renovating an existing school building. Many school buildings become educationally obsolete long before the actual structure is worn out. Such a building is a prime candidate for a renovation project if the building is still serving an adequate student population in its attendance zone. Some school systems automatically schedule a building for a renewal or renovation project when it becomes a certain age. This could be at age 25-30 years old. As a result, all school buildings in the system are maintained at a certain level of modernity.

Renovating an existing building requires a value judgment from the school board. In some ways, a renovation decision is more difficult than the decision to construct a new building in response to an increase in enrollments. Most school boards would like to make the judgment based upon a realistic assessment of the value of the building. This has to be considered in the total decision-making process, but more than likely the final decision will be more emotional than rational.

Practical Solutions

A successful renovation of an existing building is a very practical solution to the needs of the school system. Such a project can bring a community together and promote a sense of purpose and accomplishment. For these reasons, school boards seriously consider whether a renovation project is the answer to the educational needs of the school system. Such actions are never taken lightly by either school boards or governing boards.

Definitions

There are many definitions for work that is done on an existing school building to bring it up to modern standards or improve it to meet new demands. Additionally, there is no uniformity of definition across the county or even within a state for such actions or projects. What one school system might call *renewal* of a building, another school system may call a *renovation* or *rehabilitation*, where the project is the same in both instances. In some states the department of education defines what an improvement project is called, because funds for such activities come from the state. The most commonly used terms are *renovation, rehabilitation, remodeling,* and *modernization.* All four terms can and do define and describe the process of restoring a building to a standard. The *American Heritage Dictionary* (1973) gives the following definitions:

- *Renovation*—To restore to an earlier condition; improve by repairing or remodeling.

- *Remodeling*—To model again. To remake with a new structure; reconstruct; renovate.
- *Rehabilitate*—To restore to a useful life through education or therapy.
- *Modernization*—To make modern in appearance, style, or character.

As can easily be seen, the first two terms describe exactly the same process of improving the building to a previous condition. The latter two terms in the traditional sense refer to something other than buildings. Yet these terms are used in many parts of the country to describe the same improvements that the first two terms describe. There are, however, nuances among these terms, as used in the construction and design industries. Even school systems differentiate among the four terms. Probably the most popular term is renovation, which refers to those actions involved in changing and improving the physical environment of a building (Earthman, 1994). These actions endeavor to improve the structure of the building in addition to the spaces within it. The normal maintenance program of the school system may include keeping the building in as good a condition as possible, but these activities are usually accomplished over a period of years. There may or my not be any coordination of projects because the maintenance projects are designed to keep the building in working order. In a renovation project, however, improvements to all of the major systems of the building plus changes in spaces are included.

Renovation Project

A renovation project can include a complete overhaul of the building structure, the service systems (electricity, plumbing, air handling), and spaces. This would be considered a complete renovation. A partial renovation of a building might include work on selected service systems, and only certain parts of the structure. A building that has not had sufficient maintenance completed on it over a number of years would need a complete renovation at the appropriate time, whereas, a building that has had regular maintenance attention throughout its life might need only a partial renovation to bring it up to standard.

Renovation not always the answer

There are many instances where a building has been used to a point where it is not worth being renovated. Well-worn buildings may also be in areas of dwindling student population. In these circumstances, the school board and community have gotten their service out of the building, and the building might well be converted to some use other than education. The building is still a valuable community resource, but not for education. It is hard for school boards to come to this realization and act upon it, because there is always community affection for the building, and emotional ties to the structure. In these circumstances people often say, "I went there as a child and it was good enough for me, it ought to be good enough for these students." These kinds of emotions are hard to defy by abandoning the building, and citizens' groups who want the building to stay open can intimidate school board members. The result is not what is best for the students, but it does salve the emotions of the citizenry. Just as commercial and business firms depreciate their buildings and finally abandon them, so school boards need to come to the realization that the school district has gotten the completely usable life from certain buildings and must walk away from them. There is obviously no way for the school system to obtain an advantage in depreciating a school building. The net effect of moving out of a building that has served the community for a great number of years and now needs a large infusion of funds to keep it working is the same as depreciating the building.

First Choice

Renovating a school building may be the first choice of a school board or board of trustees when they are confronted with the situation of providing for additional students or changes in educational program. This is because they feel it is more economical to renovate an existing building, and students can occupy it much faster than new construction. Such beliefs are not entirely correct and are often contrary to experience. A renovation project can be more costly than new construction and take longer to complete because of unknown problems encountered during the renovation project. Each project, whether renovation or new, has its own problems. Unfortunately, the problems encountered in a renovation project may not be known before the project begins. Design professionals and engineers try to anticipate all problems in a project, whether a renovation or new construction, and take appropriate action to solve or minimize these problems.

Shortly after World War II ended, local school systems felt the crush of additional students as a result of the beginning of the first baby boom. Births began to skyrocket upon the return of service personnel. The schools tried to meet this wave of new students by constructing buildings as fast as humanly possible. Because of the dearth of quality building materials, a large number of the school buildings constructed during the period 1950–1970 were not constructed of quality material. Schools were built using less than quality material. At the turn of the 21st century, many of these buildings turned 50 years old. The normal life of a school building is between 40–50 years with proper maintenance attention. Buildings with inferior construction materials have not stood up over these years. School Boards need to make decisions regarding the continued use of these buildings. Even schools constructed with quality materials and craftsmanship do not stand up well from the constant use by students over a 50-year period of time. Keeping a school building open by renovating it or abandoning it because the school board does not want to commit sufficient funds to renovate it is a tough decision, and one that is fraught with political and emotional consequences. A primary factor is safety.

Renovation Formulas

The political and emotional forces in making a renovation decision are so strong that sometimes a decision is made regardless of the results of using a formula. Nevertheless, use of a formula helps the school board obtain data that might be useful in evaluating the results and consequences of a certain decision beforehand. Some formulas are simply rules of thumb and can only give general guidance to decision-makers. Other formulas are highly complicated and are designed to provide much more data.

Linn (1952) suggested that if a renovation project costs greater than 50 percent of what new construction would cost, it is better to go with the new construction. In fact he preferred the figure of 40 percent of the cost of new construction. These percentages are of the cost of construction of a new building, and do not include the cost of a new site.

Although this is a good guideline when considering renovation, it does not take into consideration many facets of the situation. An existing building siting on a small, constricted site in a high traffic area might not be a good candidate if the site cannot be expanded and improved. If an existing building is in a neighborhood where crime and vandalism are present, it might not be a good candidate for renovation.

Generalized Formula for School Modernization

A formula for determining the feasibility of renovating an existing building was developed by Castaldi and has been used quite extensively in school planning. The Castaldi Generalized Formula for School Modernization uses data to provide cost estimates based upon the major components of modernization such as, cost of educational, safety, and health improvements, plus site considerations (Castaldi, 1994). The formula considers a rate of depreciation and uses a hypothesis that has depreciation as the determinate. The rate of depreciation represents the funds needed to provide facilities that are adequate in every phase. Modernization of an existing building is justified if:

$$\frac{(Ce + Ch + Cs)}{(Lm)(Ia)} < \frac{R}{Lr}$$

where,

Ce = Total cost of educational improvements
Ch = Total cost for improvements in healthfulness (physical, aesthetic, and psychological)
Cs = Total cost for improvements in safety
Ia = Estimated index of educational adequacy (0–1)
Lm = Estimated useful life of the modernized school
R = Cost of replacement of school considered for modernization
Lr = Estimated life of new building (Castaldi, 1994)

The total cost of educational improvements (Ce) will include additions to the building as well as the site, special wiring for electronic technology, and even new furniture. The cost for improvements for health purposes (Ch) might include such items as a new window system, air-conditioning, resurfacing of floors, and upgrading the toilets. The cost for improvements in safety (Cs) would include making structural repairs, fireproofing stairways, repairing ceilings and roofs, and fencing for the schoolyard.

The Ia in the formula is an index of educational adequacy, or how well the building and site accommodate the educational program. This is a subjective judgment of how well the structure provides spaces that are needed by students and teachers for modern teaching/learning processes. Of course, this judgment must be made by educators based upon the proposed architectural plans and not from the actual renovated facility. It would be a good idea to have educators from outside the school system evaluate the educational adequacy of the renovation project to obtain a disinterested judgment. The type of evaluation suggested here is no different from the type of evaluation of architectural plans done for a new building. When reviewing plans for a new building, educators must project an educational program into what they see in the drawings and make determinations of the proper fit of the educational program. Many times this means judging how students will circulate inside the building.

The estimated useful life of the building (Lm) is an educated guess as to how long in the future the building will be useful to the student body and the educational program. This too is a subjective judgment made by educators based upon their thoughts regarding the stability of the student body and possible changes in educational methodology. Architects and engineers contribute historical judgments regarding the lifespan and utility of similar structures. Any evaluation should take into consideration the structural soundness of the building and how readily the building can be modified internally for future needed changes.

The symbols R and Lr stand for the cost of a new building to replace the older structure and the number of years the new building would be in use. It is assumed that maintenance costs of renovated and new buildings would be the same for the expected life of both. This may not actually be the case, because the new building would undoubtedly require less maintenance than a renovated building over the life of the building.

This formula can be used quite successfully to compare renovation versus new construction, once the appropriate data is supplied. Castaldi compares his formula with that of Linn on a hypothetical building and concludes the Linn formula is a special case of the Generalized Formula; however, the results of the two different methods probably would not coincide for a school building less than forty years old. Both of these formulas provide the school board with the tools to make a rational decision on whether to renovate. This precision adds a degree of definitiveness to the decision-making process.

There are problems in using the General Formula for School Modernization, just as there are problems in the utilization of any formula designed to provide data for a decision. The first problem deals with the ambiguity of where various renovation items may fall in the formula. For instance, the cost for installation of new carpeting may well be thought of as an educational improvement, yet it may also be a health and safety improvement. The item can be assigned to only one of the categories, however. The same conundrum can be seen with the installation of new windows. All of this points to the subjectivity of the factors entered into the formula. The last item in the formula deals with educational adequacy. This is a subjective judgment that must be quantified so as to be entered into the formula. What score one educator may assign to the educational adequacy of the proposed renovated building may be different from what another educator may assign. These numerical assignments will alter the outcome. In addition, they import an element of personal judgment, which the use of the formula was intended to reduce. Such problems do not nullify the benefits of using a formula to help in the decision-making process. The formula provides numerical measures that can be used to compare two sets of actions the school board.

Formula Limitations

As beneficial as mathematical formulas are in the decision-making process, there are limitations to their use. The formulas do not provide all of the data necessary for a sound decision. The formulas deal with costs, which is only one factor to consider when making the decision. There are others:

- Educational program requirements
- Flexibility to accommodate new teaching methods

- Educational technology requirements
- Compliance with life safety and handicap codes
- Architectural upgrading
- Asbestos abatement and other environmental requirements
- Thermal efficiency of the building environment
- Adequacy and efficiency of mechanical and electrical systems
- Adequacy of present site
- Site modification requirements
- Schedule requirements
- Current construction market
- Historical, emotional, and political issues (Earthman, 1994)

Commonwealth Renovation Assessment

Most of the foregoing factors can be re-stated in question form and quantified, to provide further data. The factors can be grouped into four large segments with

---

1. School building adaptability and condition
    ____ How well can the building accommodate new educational programs?
    ____ Can all utility systems be successfully upgraded?
    ____ Can the building be changed to comply with handicapped needs and regulations?
    ____ Is there sufficient thermal efficiency in the building envelope?
    ____ Is the building sufficiently attractive and architecturally interesting to warrant preservation through renovation or renewal?

2. School Site
    ____ It is large enough to accommodate a modern program?
    ____ Is there sufficient usable space?
    ____ Is the site located near where students live?
    ____ Is there suitable transportation available?
    ____ Is a site for a new school readily available?

3. Financial considerations
    ____ What is the cost/benefit ratio of renovating?
    ____ Is the renovation cost effective?
    ____ What is the comparison between renovation and new construction costs?

4. Political and Emotional Issues
    ____ Is the decision to renovate acceptable to the power structure and community?
    ____ Are there emotional issues tied to renovating the building?
    ____ Is there a particular community attachment to the building that would influence the decision? (Earthman, 1994).

Figure 12-1 Commonwealth Renovation Assessment.

Type of Evaluation	Components	Performed By
1. Technical survey of the facility	Architecture/structure condition Code deficiencies HVAC/electrical Site conditions Operating & maintenance costs Historic value of facility	A/E A/E A/E A/E School Staff A/E
2. Analysis of school's educational objectives	Meets educational Program Adaptability to future use Other possible uses	School Staff Sch Staff:A/E Sch Staff:A/E
3. Financial audit	Convert options to costs Relocation contingencies Evaluate operating costs Compare to new construction	School Staff School Staff School Staff School Staff
4. Examination of political climate	Predisposition of Administration Historical/sentimental value Fund raising potentia Preference for status quo Versus state-of-art	School Staff School Staff School Staff School Staff

Figure 12-2 Four-Step Evaluation for Renovation Projects.

sub-questions. An appraisal of this type can be used in conjunction with other types of assessment or formulas to provide data to the school board.

The quantification of these questions can be arranged on any scale to indicate a score from positive to negative. Although scoring these questions will provide the school board with a numerical figure, the exact meaning of the number is questionable because there is no standard to which it can be applied. The best use of this appraisal format is to permit the school board to consider all of the facets of the decision and to make the decision based upon the considered judgment of all concerned regarding the responses to the questions. Because subjective judgments must be made to determine even quantitative measures, the decision to renovate a building remains a value judgment, no matter how much numerical data is available.

Four-Step Evaluation

A four-step evaluation scheme, Figure 12-2, which is often used by architects to help explain the types of data needed and the agencies responsible for obtaining these data, has been developed. The chart expresses the type of evaluation, the components and then the agency responsible for conducting the evaluation.

School systems often employ an educational consultant to assist the school staff in conducting some of these evaluations.

An independent educational consultant, separate from the architectural firm employed by the school board, can many times provide more objective data for the school board and can advise them accordingly.

The first step in this evaluation will produce data relative to how well the building can be improved to provide service for the next several decades. This step must be completed before the rest of the evaluation can take place. Following this an evaluation must be made as to how well the building can be changed to fit a modern educational program. During the second part of this evaluation, the architect and school staff must evaluate the building to determine the proper fit for the number of students and the educational program. This is done by reviewing the initial plans developed by the architect. A detailed review of the drawings is necessary to make certain every program will have the type of space needed. After it has been determined that the proposed renovated facility will accommodate the student body and educational program, the costs and political environment must be appraised. The architect assists the school staff in determining the costs of the renovation and also in comparing these to the costs of new construction.

Process of Deciding

The first step in deciding to renovate is to assess the building for soundness and adaptability. This is done through the completion of a feasibility study. Such a study provides data regarding the need for improvement in all of the utility systems and what it will take to modify the structure to accommodate the educational program.

The starting point of the feasibility study is the development of the educational specifications that detail the educational program. This document must be prepared by the school staff and educational consultants long before the feasibility study begins. Once the educational program is translated into needed spaces and relationships, the architect and engineer can begin to make an evaluation of the building. The educational specifications are also used as an evaluative tool to assess the preliminary drawings produced by the architect.

Feasibility Study

The feasibility study is completed by the architectural firm, assisted by various consultants. The architect bases the design work on the educational program given by the school staff. This educational program is contained in a set of educational specifications that spell out in detail the type of educational program to be carried out, the number of students to be accommodated, and any special educational spaces needed. All of this description is given to the architect by the school staff for initial studies and drawings. The basic question for the architect at this time is whether or not all of the educational requirements can be fitted into the existing structure and what changes are needed to do just that. This is the crucial question for the architect and the school board and staff. The response to this question should tell the school board whether or not to go ahead with a renovation project for this building. The preliminary design review under a feasibility study will provide some conceptual ideas and sufficient analysis to estimate the costs of the renovations. This review will also enable the architect and school staff to identify any potential problems that would generate additional costs. These hidden problems can increase the total cost substantially and could limit the effectiveness of the renovation. Unfortunately, the total cost of a renovation is never known until it is completed. Feasibility studies will, however, focus the educators on how the educational program can be implemented in the renovated building rather than on the costs of the project.

There are many constraints within an existing building that can prevent the architect from providing the required spaces or certain types of spaces. These constraints might also prevent the architect from providing desired connections among academic departments within the building. Limitations include: load-bearing walls, the exterior perimeter of the building, and hidden utility service lines that may not be identified before the project began. These constraints should be specified early in the feasibility study and are to be accounted for by the architect in the cost estimate prepared for the school board.

Choosing the right course of action from a feasibility study is a difficult and complex assignment for every school board and staff. In most cases, the results of the feasibility study seems to make the options clear, but there are many confounding issues that must be dealt with by the school board. Most likely, after the school board has spent public funds on a feasibility study, they take the recommendations of the architect and school staff very seriously. This means the school staff has properly and thoroughly examined the results of the study and the suggestions are reasonable and can produce a successful renovation. Based upon these recommendations from the architect and school staff, the school board normally approves the project and directs the architect to begin the design stage of the project.

Politicization of Decision-making

As with many decisions of a school board, politics enters into the decision regarding a renovation project. Almost every decision any school board makes when dealing with school buildings, there is a political side to the question. The location of a school is usually a very volatile issue. So many times, community members may want a new school, but they do not want it on a site near them. Site selection can elicit protests. Drawing boundary lines for an attendance area is another incendiary issue that can result in stormy meetings. Renovation of an existing building is always a political flashpoint. A case in point is a school system that became embroiled in a major controversy as to whether or not to close an existing building and construct a new building. The community and school board were at loggerheads for several years before the situation was resolved. In a city on the East Coast, the school board wanted to raze an old high-school building and replace it with a new building. This would seem like an easy decision for the school board. Unfortunately, the city was still dealing with long-standing racial issues. The building proposed for replacement was a former black high school still located in the black community. The student body was approximately 85 percent black. In addition, the school was across the street from a very large low-income housing project and drew many students from that project. The site was too small for the size of the student population. Also the school was bounded on one side by a railroad track, and could not be expanded on the other sides because of housing. The school was named after a black educator, and the name had historical associations in the city. The school building was not designed for a modern educational program and contained many small instructional and laboratory areas. The physical plant was not in good condition, and asbestos was found throughout the building. In spite of this, the school building was a symbol.

An evaluation of the building by an outside educational consultant recommended the building be abandoned, because it was not serving the educational program properly and was in a very unsafe condition. When the school board took action on the report to close the high school and construct a new one, the community was incensed. Every school board meeting was the scene of demonstrations to save the building. One neighborhood association brought a speaker from outside the state to confront the school board with the demands of the community. For over three years, the project of closing the high school and constructing a new building was stalled by the political action of the neighborhood association. During a school board election the closing of the high school was a big issue and one candidate that supported closure lost the election. The new school board again took up the issue with a promise the new school would be named after the black educator and would be near the present site of the old high school. The old high school building was left standing for community use for several years after the new school was occupied.

Another case study pertains to a very economically depressed school district with a student population of approximately 4,000 students, where a large textile industry announced the closing of a factory. The factory employed a large number of workers. Previous to this, there had been a series of closings of factories by other companies. This was on top of several years of general and student population losses. As a result of this closing the county would feel a severe loss of tax revenue for the coming year. The county administrator notified the school system of a reduction of more than one million dollars in their budget for the next budgetary period. The school system had four high schools, four middle schools, and eight elementary buildings. Some of the high schools had enrollments as low as 265 students. Other schools had similar small enrollments. The school board requested a re-organization study be completed in an effort to reduce expenses. The study recommended the closure of two high schools, two middle schools, and one elementary school buildings. The elementary school was in a homogenous neighborhood. In order to complete the re-organization, several schools would need to be renovated, with costs to be born by the county government. The decision to re-organize was met with resignation in most of the communities. The community served by the elementary school to be closed was naturally not happy with the recommendations of the study and began demonstrations at school board meetings. When the school board requested funds for renovation from the county board of supervisors, the decision to re-organize the public schools essentially fell to them, because they would have to appropriate the needed funds. The dissatisfied community members demonstrated at several meetings of the county board of supervisors. Members of the county board of supervisors felt the wrath of the community because they decided not to provide the renovation funds to the school board. As a result, re-organization of the school system was impossible. The school board still needed to make-up the deficit because of the decline in tax revenues. In the budget eventually adopted by the school board, 57 teaching positions were eliminated as were several staff and custodial positions. The loss of teaching positions necessitated an increase in class size throughout the school system, and the cost of educating a student remained basically the same as before the budget reduction.

These types of political action and others similar to them happen very frequently on issues relating to school facilities. School board members must constantly face such issues in discharging their responsibility. There is not a school or workshop for school board members to learn how to handle such political questions, because each situation is unique. Resolving these situations must be learned by experience or on-the-job-training. Nevertheless, all school board members must be aware that any facility question can be politicized. School board members are elected or appointed to make policy and supervise the operation of the school system. This means the members must decide what the school system will do and how the resources of the schools will be expended. Board actions must result from serious deliberation and evaluation of the facts. Board decisions cannot be based upon popular opinion or upon the vote of the community on each issue. School board members are elected or appointed to vote in place of the community. School board members ought to have the best store of knowledge about funding. On the whole, board members are provided with technical, legal, and fiscal information that goes beyond that of the community. This information is provided in order for them to make prudent decisions on behalf of the entire community-not just on behalf of a vocal minority. The exercise of this authority sometimes sets the school board up to make an unpopular decision that could result in community dissatisfaction. Open community meetings can defuse volatile situations. Of course, a free interchange of information between the school system and local stakeholders is the best way to prevent political polarization.

References

Castaldi, B. (1994, 4th edition). *Educational facilities: Planning, Modernization, and management.* New York: McGraw-Hill, Inc.

Earthman, G. I., (1994). *School Renovation handbook: Investing in Education.* Lancaster, PA: Technomics Publishers, Inc. pp. 1–299.

Linn, H. (1952). *Modernizing School Buildings.* American School and University, 24:401.

Norris, W. (Ed.). (1973). *American Heritage Dictionary.* Boston: Houghton Mifflin Company, pp. 1–111549.

CHAPTER 13

Planning the Educational Program

Introduction

THE type of educational program offered in a school can determine the physical characteristics of the school's building. The structure's form follows education's function. Likewise, whatever is in the building in terms of furniture and equipment should also result from program demands. This premise is basic for building planning.

The same consideration holds true for the renovation of an existing school building. Two major reasons cause a school board to consider renovation: a change in the educational program that is offered and the building's age. The two reasons usually go hand-in-hand, because if a building has not been renovated or modernized for a period of time, most likely the building cannot accommodate current educational programs.

School buildings become educationally obsolete long before they become structurally obsolete. It is not an easy task to upgrade a school building to reflect program changes over a period of years. In addition, some program changes are minor enough that many school systems just make do with the existing physical surroundings. Minor changes to the structure may be completed to accommodate new needs, but little serious overall planning is usually completed due to the financial and political impediments to large-scale renovation.

When a school building is scheduled for renovation or renewal, educators have the opportunity to offer updated or new programs that may not currently exist in the school system. Renovation presents a unique chance to present a more modern educational program. Stated differently, renovation opens the door to changing the physical structure of the building to allow for new educational opportunities for students. The physical environment can be expanded to match educational ideals. This means a stretching of the minds of the faculty to

117

think in terms of new approaches and new materials. Planning should transcend how to utilize existing space.

Feasibility Study

When a new building is in the planning stage, a set of educational specifications is developed to guide the architect in the design of the structure. The building results from the educational specifications. In a renovation project, a set of educational specifications is also developed to guide the architect. The difference between the two processes is that the educational specifications for a renovation are used to help the architect complete a feasibility study upon which a decision will be made. This study is completed before the actual decision to go forward with the renovation takes place. The results of the feasibility study provide the school board with the information to make a decision. In other words, the feasibility study lets the educators and school board know how well the building can be changed to accommodate the program and how these changes are to be accomplished. At the same time, the study also informs them of limitations and compromises that must be made to continue to use the building. They have to consider whether or not the limitations and compromises are sufficiently large enough to make the renovation less cost-effective than new construction. This is vastly different from the decision to construct a new building and requires much more consideration as to the quality of the end product. The decision is based upon how well the renovated building can accommodate the educational program.

There are many situations where the only option open to the school board is to renovate. No site may be available for new construction, or the financial resources of the school system are such that new construction can not be an option, or the political climate is not friendly to new construction outlays. Even in these situations, the school board should have a feasibility study completed by an architect. Educators still need to know how well a renovated facility can fit the program and what limitations and compromises they will need to make. In addition, the school board must have the cost projections from the study.

Educational Specifications

The most important task to be done when considering a renovation project or a new building project is to adequately describe the activities and needs of the users of the facility. The needs of the users will include the kinds and types of spaces, their location, furniture, and equipment. Details about such items are embodied in a set of educational specifications.

Writing a set of educational specifications is a comprehensive task and is the responsibility of those in the district who supervise and deliver instruction. Others lack the necessary experiential and knowledge base for the task. The person responsible for producing a set of educational specifications must have sufficient time. Some school systems release a principal from administrative responsibility to work full-time on educational specifications. Many school systems employ an outside educational consultant to work with the staff to produce such a document. Outside consultants can bring a certain amount of objectivity to the process, but should not impose educational change upon the faculty. An educational consultant should bring fresh ideas to the school system for consideration by the faculty and administration. Whether or not these ideas are implemented is left to the school system. The interchange between educational consultant and faculty should produce a lively discussion of ideas. Through exchanging ideas, the faculty should be able to review what they are currently doing and whether or not they wish to change the instructional program.

In a renovation project, it might be difficult for the faculty to see the possibilities in changing the spaces and layout in the existing building. The renovation should not be cosmetic only, e.g., interior repainting and furniture upgrades. For teachers who have been in the building for a number of years, it might be difficult to imagine changes to the structure of a building. This is not unusual. For this reason, a consultant can be engaged to push the faculty to think beyond their present building. In working with a faculty, a consultant might want to start with a blank sheet of paper and get the faculty to think about what they want to do as far into the future as they can see. The consultant might use presentations by other educators regarding new programs that have been successfully implemented, brainstorming sessions, visits to other schools, and self-examination exercises to assist the faculty to think about the future and what they want it to be in the renovated facility. A faculty might reaffirm the existing program but still need expanded spaces in which to conduct the program. The process of developing a set of specifications does not necessarily mean that the educational program will change noticeably. If the school has an exciting educational program that reflects new instructional strategies and materials and meets the needs of the students, there is little reason for change. The self-evaluation process that normally takes place in developing educational specifications is beneficial in and of itself. Following such re-examination, a faculty can enter into the renovated facility with renewed strength and vigor. If this happens, the renovation has been a success. The end-product of these activities is documented in a set of educational specifications that give detailed advice to the architect. The architect uses this document first of all to complete the feasibility study. Later, after the decision to renovate has been made, the architect will use it to design the renovation.

In the feasibility document, the educational program is defined quite specifically down to the kinds of courses that will be offered and the types of spaces these courses will need. The relationship of these spaces to one another is described. The number and ages of students to be housed are identified, along with any special needs. The number, types, and kinds of furniture and equipment that will be needed are listed. All of these descriptions are included in a complete set of educational specifications. Some of the subjects covered in a good set of educational specifications might include:

- Description of the Community
- Description of the Student Population
- Educational Program & Courses
- Site Description and Equipment
- Traffic and Parking
- General Instructional Areas Needed
- Space Requirements
- Specific Instructional Areas Needed
- Area Relationships
- Equipment Needed
- Building Communications and Utilities
- Plant Security
- Plant Service Areas and Facilities

The educational specifications provide a detailed description of two very important processes that take place simultaneously in the classroom. There are certain activities in which students engage to learn the knowledge, skills, and attitudes offered in the curriculum. These activities could include sitting at a desk, lying on the floor, meeting in groups, dancing, running, and singing, manipulating objects, operating equipment, writing on a chalkboard or whiteboard, or even planting seeds. For instance, on the primary level, the teacher wants to read to the students. The students need a space in which to sit in a small group and perhaps on the floor. A high-school teacher may wish to have a small group of students present a sketch explaining a poem. Both of these activities are essential to learning. Students are active during the entire school day in some form or the other. As a result of these activities, planned physical elements, spaces, and accoutrements are needed to support the learning activity.

At the same time as the students are engaged in directed and free learning activities, the teacher has a set instructional agenda. The process of teaching requires the teacher to do certain things to present material to the students. The teacher may engage in lecturing, discussing, showing, writing, observing, talking, or any other kind of activity that is required to help students learn. As such, the teacher needs certain spaces, equipment, and accoutrements.

The confluence of these two processes is where the heart of the educational program is located. The educational specifications relate the program to spaces, spatial relationships, and equipment within the building. The physical environment must accommodate and support teaching and learning as it is done and planned for.

A set of educational specifications for a renovation project is no different from those for a new building. Existing buildings, however, may put more constraints upon the wishes and needs of the students and teachers. For this reason, more compromises may have to be made. Existing buildings may have immoveable load-bearing walls that in turn limit the creation of new spaces. They may also limit the amount of change that can be made in the building, or limit the implementation of certain instructional programs. For instance, a popular organizational scheme involves creating smaller groups of students to be housed in a specific area of the buildings. These schemes are variously called a *school-within-a-school*, the *house concept*, or *school centers*. The idea behind this plan is to divide the total student population into small groups to be located in one area of the building. In new buildings, this may be a cluster of classrooms where all of the major subjects such as English, social studies, mathematics, and science are taught by a teaching team. The teachers and students stay together most of the day for instructional purposes. The only time students leave the "house" is for specialized instruction in such subjects as physical education, music, art, foreign language, or another special subject. To implement this concept fully, instructional spaces need to be clustered, along with support facilities such as conference rooms, teacher offices, storage areas, and restrooms. The scheme requires considerable space, even if the number of students is not large. In older buildings the classrooms are often strung out along a corridor that serves as a main circulation area. Obviously with this kind of linear configuration, it is difficult to establish a sense of a house organization and feeling on the part of students of being in a single space as one group. As a result, capturing space where a number of classrooms can be clustered is virtually impossible, and the architect is challenged to provide a usable physical solution.

Development Responsibility

The responsibility of developing the educational program rests with the school system employees. One person or office should be charged with the obligation of actually developing and writing the educational specifications. This individual is usually called an educational planner. This single point of responsibility serves to make a more concise document and assures final completion in a timely fashion. The person or office should assume the duty of gathering all of the data from the various groups and individuals who will be involved in the process of deciding on the educational program. The individual charged with the duty of actually writing the specifications may be a school system employee or an outside educational consultant. For a renovation project, the principal of the school would be an ideal person to head this part of the project. The principal should be released from the actual day-by-day administration of the school to devote full time to the writing of educational specifications, for the follow-up review of architectural plans, and subsequent planning during the renovation activities. Outside educational consultants can assist the principal in the writing process, but the principal should head the development of the educational specifications. The obligation of this person or office is to make certain all interested groups and individuals have input into the document through whatever means. The person in charge of this process will want to meet with all of these interests. There may be group meetings for teachers and parents. Other individuals, such as the director of maintenance and operations or food service, should be interviewed in person.

Process Involvement

Three major groups are involved in renovation planning. The first group is the faculty and staff who are currently working in the building. The second group should be those central administration specialists that have expertise and responsibility in certain areas or subjects. These might include curriculum specialists, librarians, vocational education supervisors, directors of maintenance and operations, transportation, and food service directors. The third major group is representatives of the larger community. In some instances, school systems involve students in the process of developing educational specifications. Many times the involvement of parents, students, and community members serves more of an educative process for them than securing actual input on educational needs. Involving parents in a renovation project is also important because it tells the parents and others the school board is interested enough in the community to upgrade and improve the school building which in turn reflects well upon the neighborhood. Involvement in the planning process will also engender the good will of the parents and community members. This may be needed in case the school board must pass a bond referendum to pay for the renovation.

The first meeting of interested parties should define the role of the planner and the responsibility for completing a document that incorporates the desires and needs of the students and teachers. The first part of the process of obtaining data is fact finding, where groups and individuals are asked what they desire in the renovated facility. Some of the wishes may not be affordable. For instance, often during the planning for a high school, groups may suggest convincingly the need for a swimming pool, yet such a facility is typically not within the scope of the project in the planning of the school board. Such differences must be reconciled during the course of interchanges in some fashion by the planner, so that a document acceptable to the school board may be finalized.

The various groups and individuals in the planning process should be identified by the school personnel. The principal should have a large part in suggesting and determining community groups for involvement. In this way, no community individual or group is left out. At the same time, the central administration should suggest groups and individuals on a larger scale to be included. No group or individual should be left out of planning, but the number of groups and individuals should not be so large that the planning process is bogged down. A representative of a group should be sent to the planning activities, but not the entire group.

Document Review

The review process of the proposed document should include those individuals in responsible positions within the school system to make certain all segments and departments of the school system are kept informed of the progress. The reviews should take place periodically to insure continuity. In this manner, when the final document is completed, everyone will know its contents.

In a school system with more than one building, there may be some general parameters that all buildings share. The parameters may be related to certain educational program requirements that should be implemented. For instance, the school system might want every school to have the same size library, based upon student population. A school system might want every elementary school building to contain a full-sized gymnasium for community use. Some school systems have a uniform type of heating plant for every building, and these must be specified in the document.

At the completion of the document review, a final reading of the manuscript should be made for approval purposes. All of the groups and individuals that participated in the development should be included in this final gesture, especially the decision-makers in the school system. Although this review should be routine, it provides closure to the development of the educational specifications.

Following this, the school board should review the document, and formally vote on it in regular meeting. It is important that this take place, because the educational specifications will function as the ultimate criteria in all questions regarding the design of the renovation project. Board approval standardizes the requirements for the renovation project and limits the expansion of the scope of work.

In a renovation project, the set of educational specifications is given to the school board appointed architect, who will then prepare the feasibility study. During the work of developing the feasibility study, the architect should confer with the appropriate persons designated as the reviewers of the work. The reviewers would include the principal and representatives of the faculty and staff. If the school system employs an individual to serve as the educational planner, that person should be involved in all meetings with the architect.

The architect should meet frequently during the stage of preparing the feasibility study with the above members of the review panel. In this manner, the review panel can provide significant input regarding the ideas the architect has put forth. The give and take of these review sessions should provide for a good resolution of the problems the architect faces in trying to accommodate the needs of the school system in the existing building. The completed feasibility study, along with sketches of the suggested changes to the structure of the building, should result from this review process and be approved by the panel. The feasibility study should be presented to the school board, along with estimates of what the project should cost. Based upon the sketches, the narrative of the study, and the cost estimates, the school board will make their decision whether or not to proceed. Where a decision must be made between renovation and new construction, the school board will want to know the pros and cons of both. They also will need to know the cost benefit between the two choices. Where it has been decided to renovate, the school board needs to know the costs. If the costs of renovation are beyond the school board, adjustments must be made before decisions to go ahead are made.

Completion of the feasibility study is in a manner of speaking similar to the completion of the schematic drawings architects develop for a new school project. The schematic design is a milestone for the development of the plans for the new school and they are presented to the school board for their approval. Based upon the approval of the school board, the architect can proceed to design development and completion of the design documents. If the schematic design and accompanying cost estimates are beyond the means of the school board, adjustments have to be made before the architect can proceed with design development.

When the sketches of the renovation and cost estimates are approved, the architect will proceed to develop the final drawings. This stage of development is crucial to both the architect and school system, because this is the period when decisions are made that cannot be reversed without considerable expense. Careful review of the development of the drawings must be adhered to, so that both architect and school system can be assured the design is in accordance with the educational specifications and will accommodate the school needs.

References

Earthman, Glen I. (1976). *The process of developing educational specifications.* Blacksburg, VA: College of education, Virginia Polytechnic Institute and State University.

Graves, B. E. (1993). *School ways: The planning and design of America's schools.* New York: McGraw-Hill, Inc.

Hawkins, H. (1991). "Developing educational specifications," Unit F, *Guide for Planning Educational Facilities.* Scottsdale, AZ: Council of Educational Facility Planners, international.

Herman, J. J. & Herman, J. L. (1995). *Effective school facilities: A development guidebook.* Lancaster, PA: Technomic Publishing Company.

Mackenzie, D. G. (1989). *Planning educational facilities.* Lanham, MD: University Press of America.

CHAPTER 14

Selection of the Architect

Introduction

ONE of the most important decisions a school board must make in renovating an existing school building is deciding what architectural firm will be selected for the project. Whatever efforts the school board and staff put into the selection process to obtain good architectural assistance is rewarded hundreds of times over in a product that is very useful to the teachers, administrators, support staff, and students. The architect is the individual who will translate the needs of the users of the building into a finished product.

When employing an architect for a new school building, almost all districts require that the successful applicant have experience in designing the type of school building needed. If the project is a high school, the successful architect applicant will have had experience with this level of educational building. Likewise, if a special building such as a vocation education facility or a special-needs facility is to be designed, architects must have the experience. In renovation projects, the same requirement is of even more importance. Renovation projects are much more complicated than new construction, because of possible hidden problems. In addition, an architect must work with more limitations in a renovation project than for new construction.

Method of Selection

There are three methods for selecting an architect for any kind of capital project: direct or non-competitive, competitive review, and design competition selection. There may be some variation in how these methods are employed on the local scene, but basically, architects, just as any other professionals, are selected through either some sort of competitive selection or directly without the necessity of competition.

Direct Selection

Whenever a school board offers a commission for work to an architect without considering other architects, they are using the direct method of selection. This method is used frequently in small school systems or in small communities with limited sources of architectural services. This method of selection also presupposes the architect is familiar with the buildings in the school system. Many times school boards feel more comfortable re-employing the same architect for multiple projects, because the architect is familiar with all the buildings in the district. For renovation projects, this might be a benefit.

The mechanics for selection and subsequent employment of an architect under this method is for the superintendent to contact the architect to arrange a meeting with the school board to outline the project. If the architect is currently under contract with the school board, there could be an extension of an existing contract, especially if the project is very small and closely related to the project in which the architect is currently engaged. Conceivably, an architect that has not worked for the school system can be contacted for selection. In these situations, the superintendent in all likelihood has heard about the architect from other superintendents or trusted sources. This method of selecting an architect is probably used more often than one thinks. The method is definitely less costly than any other. It is a rapid method for obtaining architectural services when needed and where the architect may know the physical plant well. In addition, there might be a modified fee for repeated commissions.

Nonetheless, the direct method of selection has several disadvantages. With repeated commissions in one school system, there is a danger that the same architectural solution to building problems may be used over and over again. Using one architect may mean that all buildings look alike and have stock mechanical systems. If there are any problems, they will be repeated in every building. Using a variety of architects brings unique solutions to architectural problems and provides variety in the buildings. Of absolute importance is the fact that architectural services should be selected based upon qualifications rather then friendship.

Competitive Review

In some states, local school systems are required to secure professional services through a competitive process of review of qualifications. A sole source of services must be documented and justified, before a contract can be offered. This would apply also to obtaining architectural services. This provision guarantees a safety net for the superintendent and school board in selecting the architect.

In private and parochial school systems, the process of selecting an architect may use the direct or non-competitive method. There are several considerations to be observed in this regard. In some church-related schools, a member of the church who is an architect may be asked to accept the commission, because the school administration believes that person is familiar with the workings of the school and can satisfy the needs of the school. This may well be an advantage to the school. Likewise, in the private school sector there may be an architect in the community, who would be willing to accept a commission. In both of these situations, the architect should have considerable experience in renovating existing facilities before being employed. If the person does not have such experience, the school authorities should publicly advertise for architectural services in the same manner the public schools advertise, so as to obtain an architect with such experience. In developing the process of selection, the private and parochial schools should strongly consider the use of an educational consultant, because of the limitation of staff personnel.

Design Competition

This method of selecting an architect utilizes a design problem that an architect solves to secure consideration for a commission. Under this method, a school system prepares a set of educational specifications or a description of the project under consideration. Architects can be either asked by the school board to apply for the competition or can apply themselves, depending upon whether or not the competition is open or closed. The educational specifications are supplied to the architects to use in solving the architectural solution to the project. The architects in the competition then complete preliminary drawings and elevations of at least the front of the building and perhaps major areas. The drawings are usually line drawings of various components of the building, mainly to show relationships. These documents are submitted to the school board, which evaluates them. Selection of the successful architect is based upon this evaluation.

This method of selecting an architect may sound promising and exciting, yet there are more disadvantages to it than there are advantages. The disadvantages apply to both school system and architect. The main disadvantage for an architect is that he or she must invest a considerable amount of funds in the beginning with only a chance of recouping the investment. If the architect is successful, the initial investment becomes part of the negotiated fee for design of the building. If the architect is not successful, the initial investment is a direct loss and usually cannot be recovered. Even if the architect is successful in winning the competition, the school system may require quite a few changes in the plans submitted, thereby creating a larger investment of funds at this point of initial development than would be desirable. There are also disadvantages for the school system. In the usual course of a design competition, the work of the architect is independent of advice from the staff of the school system. As a result, there is no input by school system employees in the initial phase of design development. One of the most important periods in the design stage is the conceptualizing of the building done by the architect. This period of design should have early and regular input from the school staff to avoid costly mistakes, which will turn up later in the design stage. The architect also needs this input to make certain the design is true to the educational specifications. Without this assistance, the architect must translate the educational specifications alone. The design concept may be what the school system needed and wanted, but then it may not meet all of the needs and desires of the school staff. In this case, it may be very difficult to change the design concept because the architect has bought into the concept and does not want to change it. Considerable difficulty for both the architect and school system can result from this situation.

Sometimes the design concept selected is the one that appeals to the aesthetic side of those doing the judging, and not to the practical side of configuring the internal structure of the building. The most important aspect of a building is how it works for the users of the structure, and in most cases this has very little to do with the aesthetics of the building. The internal relationships of the various components of the building are one of the most important parts that make it successful. Consideration of these relationships may be lost in the evaluation of which design looks best. In addition, the judges, if they are lay persons, may not be the users of the building and must make judgments based upon something other than a first hand knowledge of the needs of the users.

This method of selecting an architect consumes a great deal of time on the part of the school system staff in preparing the educational specifications and preparing for the competition. It is not a very cost-effective method of selecting an architect. Few school systems use this method, because it is so cumbersome. Only in those situations where there is either an historical building that needs to be renovated or a prestigious school needs to be designed is this method used.

Review of Applicants

The most popular method of selecting an architect is the competitive review of applicants. This method is very much like employing any professional to do work for the school system. The competitive method can be rather lengthy and involved, but the end result is well worth the effort. This method also engenders better relations with the world of the design professionals than either of the other two methods. Architects feel they have an equal opportunity to receive a commission based upon their previous work and knowledge of the process. This makes for a level playing field for everyone, and the major beneficiary is the school system.

Developing a Selection Process

The competitive selection of design professionals is a simple matter, yet requires considerable investigation on the part of the school system staff. Several steps have to be taken, which deal with the people who should be involved, the degree of involvement, the criteria to be used for selection, the materials to be evaluated, the method of evaluation, and the final determination. The school staff should develop the process to be used and present it to the school board for approval. This will insure an objective and bias-free selection process.

In large school systems that have multiple renovation projects in the works, the process is routine. In school systems that do not have a multitude of projects, a process is not in place, and the school staff must develop one. Normally an administrator in the business section of the school system will be given the responsibility of developing a selection process. The process should be informed by school board policies on employment of outside professional expertise and school personnel selection. In some states, the procurement policies of the state will dictate the process. In all circumstances, the approved process should address the following questions:

- What person or office will be responsible for administering the process?
- Who will be involved in the process?
- What criteria will be used?
- What office/person will make the recommendation to the school board?

The resolution of these questions is important to insure an orderly and successful selection process.

Who Is Involved?

One of the first questions in developing a selection process is to decide who will be involved. In a large school system, this is a difficult question, because many individuals feel they should be involved. A larger issue governing involvement of individuals is: What expertise does a person bring to the process that would require their attendance? This question is related to hiring laws. Employing an architect is a personnel matter, and there are certain employment protocols and guidelines that must be observed, so that privacy issues are not compromised. In addition, the more individuals involved in the process, the more cumbersome and lengthy it becomes. Large committees do not make the process any better and might be more costly to the school system. As a result, the selection process should involve a very small number of school system employees.

In a small school system, those involved might include the assistant superintendent for business/operations, the director of maintenance, and someone from the instructional section of the school organization. In a renovation project, the principal of the school to be renovated and at least one of the faculty members should also be included in this group. The same configuration of individuals should apply to private and parochial schools. Again, in small private/parochial schools, the need for educational consultant assistance is very evident in this matter.

It has become popular to involve parents in various efforts of the educational process. The same criteria for involvement in the architectural selection process that applies to staff members in the school system apply to parents and lay persons. If they bring some expertise to the process, there is a possibility of inclusion. Absent this, parents and laypersons should not be involved in the selection of the architect. The school staff members who will be working with the architect during the design stage should be the ones involved in the process. All other individuals and groups should be excluded. This way there cannot be any question regarding the legality of the process.

Criteria Development

The first task of the committee charged with selecting the architect is to develop criteria to be used in the selection process. At first this may seem like a tremendous job for the group, but there are guidelines that can be of assistance in developing criteria. All criteria should help the committee properly evaluate individuals in a fair manner. In addition, the criteria must always relate directly to the task to be done by the successful candidate. Some criteria are required by state law, such as architectural registration. Other criteria relate directly to the quality of work done by the architect. These latter criteria are more difficult to evaluate, but judgments need to be made based upon the best available evidence.

One school system established the following criteria to be used for the initial review and screening of architectural firms for renovation projects.

- Prior experience with renovations
- An understanding of the state department of education procedures
- Quality of prior work
- Project team experience
- Ability to perform on time
- Ability to be on site daily
- Past commitment to EEO and minority business partnerships (Earthman, 1994)

Each staff reviewer was to rate the firms based upon these criteria using weighted maximum scores for a total of 100 points. The architectural firm that scored the highest on these criteria was then recommended to the school board for approval and a commission.

Other more traditional criteria deal with the background of the architect, professional activities, location of offices, staffing, references, and interest in the project.

Registration and Professional Activities

All architects must be licensed or registered in the state in which they are working. This registration is achieved by completing an accredited architectural program at a college or university. This program includes courses leading to the degree and internships with architectural firms. Next, the architect must pass an examination. Registration certifies that the architect is approved by the state to provide architectural services. Every architect must place a seal on all completed work that includes the registration number. In this manner the school knows the work was done by a person approved by the state (Vickery, 1998).

Registration is granted on a state-by-state basis, and an architect from out of the state must gain registration in the state where work is to be done. In some cases, out-of-state architects will partner with a local architectural firm and use the registration of the local architect for the work to be done. The local architect becomes the architect of record, but the out-of-state architect may do the major share of the design work.

Architects can be recognized by their professional organization for outstanding work in their field by gaining membership in the American Institute of Architects (AIA). Such membership indicates recognition by the profession of individually outstanding work, and is shown by the initials AIA following the name of the architect. A further distinction of outstanding work is election to the College of Fellows of the AIA (FAIA).

An architect may belong to the Council of Educational Facility Planners, International. This organization is composed of educators, consultants, professors, architects, and equipment vendors interested in school facility design. Membership in this organization indicates to the school board that the person is interested in keeping abreast of trends in educational facilities.

Another standard that can be used for this criterion is that of design awards for outstanding school projects. The following groups have award competitions for outstanding work: the American Association of School Administrators (AASA); Association of School Business Officials, International (ASBO); the Council of Educational Facility Planners, International (CEFPI); and the Association of Physical Plant Administrators (APPA). Even state educational facility planner associations have such awards. Annually these organizations hold a competition and award recognition for outstanding projects. The school system should evaluate all of these forms of recognition.

Experience in Renovation Work

The history of an architectural firm is important to the school system because it tells them the nature and number of the projects in which members of the firm have been engaged. The quality of the work experience is one thing, but if the school system is looking for an architect with considerable experience in renovation or remodeling, this fact should show in the work history. The work history should give the school system staff a good idea of types of renovation problems the architect has faced and the solution to the problem. Although no two renovation projects are the same, there are certain things a school staff should look for.

One of the most perplexing problems associated with renovating older buildings is the presence of asbestos. The presence of asbestos can be a costly item in a renovation project. How an architect anticipated such a problem before beginning and how the problem was solved are good indicators of the experience of the architect. The number and amount of any cost overruns is also an important indicator of either good or poor planning. The degree of satisfaction with the project on the part of the school staff using the building is another benchmark for project success.

If the school system staff is seeking architectural expertise in a renovation project for a middle school, they want the architect to have some experience with middle school renovations. The work history will provide such information. An additional concern might be that although the architectural firm has a good deal of renovation experience, the person assigned the project may have little or no firsthand experience in a renovation. The school system wants to make certain the principal architect on their project is the one with the experience listed. This provision or guarantee can be worked into the contract the architectural firm signs.

Method of Operation and Knowledge of DOE Regulations

Working with school systems is considerably different from working with non-governmental clients. There are several reasons for this. In the first place, an educational facility is a specialized and complicated structure. Without experience in designing a school building, architects find there are many local, state, and federal regulations that must be observed. The first time an architect begins designing an educational facility, a great deal of time will need to be spent to research these regulations and guidelines, to obtain approval by various boards and offices. Sometimes, this research effort can delay a project.

An educational facilities project requires many more official approvals than other types of design projects. These approvals are both within and outside the school system. The approvals within the school system deal more with the design of the project. Approvals from outside of the school system normally deal with structural and materials problems and issues. This is where prior knowledge of the requirements of the state department of education and other state agencies is extremely important

Educational facility projects require the architect to make presentations to many groups of individuals, both school staff and community lay persons. Although this is not an intimidating prospect in and of itself, the architect must make these presentations and then take the input and try to make sense out of perhaps conflicting requests. The architect must be able to ascertain the need and propriety of such requests and still deliver to the school system the design needed. This aspect of design work is quite different from ordinary design projects, such as office buildings or homes, and presents quite a challenge to the ability of the architect.

Quality of Previous Work

This criterion refers to how well the architect performed on other design work. This might be a rather subjective judgment, but one way to find out how successful the architect was is to ask the present users of the building, regardless of whether it is a renovation project, an addition, or a new building. This is the most telling data regarding the worth of an architect. When users of the building are asked if it is a successful building project, their answer should be an unswerving affirmative. One must use caution, however, in assessing some of the comments of the users, and evaluators should look for answers to specific questions raised.

Staff and Offices

School authorities want to make certain the staff and technical assistance behind the architect is sufficient to permit the project to be completed in a satisfactory manner in the scheduled period of time. The architect is extremely important in the design work for an educational project, but the individuals that provide the technical and clerical support are equally important. The school staff should visit the offices of the architectural firm to see firsthand that such support is readily available for the project. The school staff should also make an assessment of the use of technology for the design of the building. For example, Computer Aided Design Development (CADD) systems should be readily available for all phases of design conceptualization and development. Although the assessment of the office of the architect is a subjective judgment, school staff members must be assured in some manner, through the visit, that the best people and the most advanced technology will be employed on their project.

Interest in the Project

The school board wishes to employ an architect that is vitally interested in the project. The school staff needs to determine if the project will receive the highest priority in the work of the architectural firm. The principal of the firm should provide the school board with reasonable assurance the project will receive priority. Judgments regarding the interest an architectural firm may have for school projects can be obtained through interviews and subsequent discussions about the work. Architects believe a school commission is very desirable because of the stability of the school system and the assurance of prompt payments.

References

The architectural firm may give several kinds of references. Some references will be for design work completed previously, and even for the credit worthiness and stability of the firm. The latter references are very important for the school board, because they want to employ a firm that will be able to carry a renovation project through to the end without any financial problems. For almost every architectural firm, this kind of assessment is in effect pro forma.

The references regarding the quality of work performed by the architect are important for the assessment of client satisfaction. These references should be contacted for an evaluation of the kind of work performed. Each architect will provide a list of renovation projects completed. The users of these buildings should be interviewed to find their reaction to the finished product. All of these sources of information should provide the school staff with data to form a strong impression. The basic questions that need answers are:

- How well did the architect respond to the needs of the school system?
- How cooperative were members of the architectural firm?
- Did the firm stay within the budget?
- How many *change orders* were performed and for how much?
- Did the architect maintain the approved calendar so that the completion was timely?
- How serviceable is the final product - the building?
- Would you re-employ the architect for another renovation project? (Earthman, 2000).

All of the above criteria should be used to obtain information necessary to make a recommendation to the school board to either employ or not to employ the architect.

Selection Process

The school system notifies the public that it is interested in securing architectural expertise in the design of a capital improvement project. This can be done in several ways. If the request is sent out through a Request for Proposals (RFP), public notification as described in the legal code must be observed. The school system can send such notice to the state chapter of the American Institute of Architects. The AIA in turn notifies its members of the RFP so that each member can respond if interested. State legal code may require public notification in the legal newspaper of the locality. Additionally, each state department of education maintains a list of architects who design buildings and will share that with the local school system. The goal of the school system is to make as broad a notification as possible. In this manner, the best architectural firm will be selected from a large number of inquiries.

The initial notification may well take the form of a letter of invitation or in the case of a legal notice, a standardized form requesting proposals. Regardless of the form of the notification, it should contain certain information the architect needs in order to make a decision whether or not to apply for consideration. The basic information should include: the type of project (new or renovated construction), general scope of the work to be done, educational level of the building, number of students to be served, location of the site, schedule for the project, type and kind of information that is to be submitted to the school board, dates for submission of material, and address where material should be sent.

Based upon this information, an architect should be able to decide whether or not to apply for consideration. Once the decision is made, the architect must assemble all of the material requested by the school system. The material will usually reflect the types of educational projects that have been completed, the location of these facilities, some cost data, a list of references, location of offices, and an expression of interest and availability. The school system may specify other material that might explain the ability of the architect. This could include credit references for the firm to determine stability. The school system may also want to know if the architect will be subcontracting professional services such as engineering, lighting, and plumbing. If so, the architect will want to list the specific sub-contractors and their expertise. More and more, school systems are requiring architectural firms to have educational planning expertise on the staff. An educational consultant is one who has had experience in the school setting and has planning expertise. Educational planning expertise is quite different from professional design expertise and relates closely to that phase of the project dealing with the needs of the educational program and the faculty. Again, if such expertise is not on the staff, the school system will want to know who will be doing this phase of work. This is the material the school staff will consider in trying to reduce the number of potential architect to a reasonable number for the short list. Usually a school system will want to select 3 to 5 firms to be on the short list to be interviewed. The material is reviewed by the school system staff to make the decision as to which firms will be on the list to be interviewed.

Evaluating Credentials

Prima facie, it may appear incongruous to have educators evaluate the material sent in by the architect, since this entails one professional group evaluating the work of the professionals in a different discipline. Such evaluation, however, is very commonly used because the educators are in actuality the users of the product of the architect and have knowledge of what is needed. As such, the educators are experts in making recommendations to the school board of architectural firms for their consideration.

In addition to reviewing the material submitted by the architect, the school review staff will want to investigate three other sources of valuable information to be used in the selection process. Each architectural applicant will supply the school board with a list of completed projects that are similar to the one under consideration. If the project is a renovation or modernization of an existing building, the project should demonstrate that kind of work. The school staff should plan to visit at least one of these renovated projects to see what the building is like and to interview the users of it. The staff should observe the type of materials used in the renovation, the amount of space devoted to the instructional process as compared to the amount of non-instructional space, the flow of traffic, and how the renovation was carried out. This kind of information should provide a basis for judging what to expect from the architect as far as the building characteristics are concerned. These are crucial items in making the building a success and should show the ability of the architectural firm to produce a successful renovation project.

User Evaluations

Information can be secured from the users of the building about how user-friendly the building is and if the users consider the building to be successful. An interview with selected users of the building will give the staff some insights as to how well the building serves the needs of the users. The interview can also disclose informal data about the quality of the building.

Site Visits

The third source of information is a visit to the offices and work places of the architectural firm. The purpose of this visit is to see the extent of the staff and the projects on which they are currently working. Architects welcome such visits, which give them an opportunity to showcase the expertise found in the staff, as well as outline how a project is developed and completed in the office.

After all of the material and information are assembled and reviewed, the school staff must make a recommendation to the school board for the short list, based upon their evaluation. Almost all of the information is subjective. This is not a disadvantage because the statements of the users of a building the staff visited should provide rather good insight into the work of the architect. In addition, the information gathered as a result of the visit to the building, should enable the staff to form impressions, which will affect the eventual selection.

The school staff, however, should develop a form of evaluation that will result in the selection of the 3–5 architectural firms that best meet the needs of the school system.

School Board Interview

In some very unusual instances in small school systems, the school board interviews all of the architectural firms that have sent in material and want to be considered. This may result in interviewing as many as 10–15 firms. This is a terrible waste of time and money for both the school system and the architects. In addition, the situation is rife with the possibilities of wrong decisions. Interviewing that many firms will present the school board with an overload of information and not sufficient time to consider all of the data. Small school systems may try to justify such actions as a necessity because of a lack of adequate school professional staff. The lack of sufficient professional staff is a reality in many small school systems; however, this can be partly remedied through consultants. The costs to employ an educational consultant to review the applications and make a recommendation to the school board, is more than offset by the expense of reading the material sent to the school board and interviewing a large number of firms. Choosing the best firms and making an intelligent decision based upon a consultant's recommendation far outweigh the time and effort of interviewing many firms and not making a decision based upon sound information.

The architectural firms selected for the short list are then interviewed and permitted to make a short presentation to the school board and school staff. At the interview, architects like to introduce their staff and all of the major players who will be working on the project. The presentation usually focuses on two main ideas. The first is the expertise of the firm, which is conveyed by displaying recent projects. Pertinent data on each building project such as building costs and length of time of the project are presented to the school board. The second major idea relates to how members of the firm plan to work with the staff and community. This is an important consideration for both the architect and the school board, especially if the school board is desirous of community involvement in the planning process. The school board wants to know how members of the firm will interact with staff and community members.

Employing the Architect

Based upon this interview/presentation and the material submitted previously, the school board makes a decision to employ one of the firms. The school board or governing body should pass a resolution to contract with the selected architectural firm. Following this, the legal counsel for the school system executes a contract with the principal of the firm, which then moves to design work.

References

Earthman, G. I. (2000). *Planning educational facilities for the next century.* Reston, VA: Association of School Business Officials, International.

Graves, B. E. (1993). *School ways, the planning and design of America's schools.* New York: McGraw-Hill, Inc.

Holcomb, J. H. (1995). *A guide to the planning of educational facilities.* 3rd edition, Lanham, MD: university Press of America.

Vickery, R. L. (1998). *Finding the right architect.* Charlottesville, VA: The Thomas Jefferson Center for Educational Design, University of Virginia.

CHAPTER 15

What the Architect Does

THE architect is responsible for all of the design work necessary to construct a structure. Further, the architect is responsible for some supervision of the project during the construction phase and to furnish certification that the building is completed. Staff architects provide design services for small projects within the school system or for supervision of architects who are employed by the school board.

- Architects are normally employed for the following basic services:
- schematic design
- design development
- contract document development
- bidding advisement
- construction monitoring

Architects can provide other services such as pre-planning, site evaluation, feasibility studies, programming activities, and orientation to the building. All of these activities are outside of the basic services covered in the architectural contract, and are secured at extra cost to the school system (Graves, 1993).

Architectural firms may provide educational consultant services as part of the total services stipulated within the contract they sign. This is an excellent way for the school system to obtain needed educational planning expertise. The cost of such consultation is borne by the architectural firm, but is contained within the total fees paid to the architect. Some school systems may believe such services are gratis, because they do not directly pay for such services. They are not. Whatever additional services the school system needs should be discussed and decided upon at the time of the contract negotiations, so that the responsibility for the cost can be determined and the school system does not have any expectations for services that will not be provided in the basic contract. One of the most controversial subjects in negotiating with the architect is the degree of supervision the architect will provide for the construction phase. Most school systems desire daily supervision of construction activities. That condition, plus its costs, must be specified in the contract. The school system may also opt to have one of its own employees supervise construction.

Schematic Design Development

In the initial stage of the project, an architect develops a schematic concept for the building and works to place all of the components within the structure, observing proper relationships between the components. The concept results from not only the educational program to be offered in the building, but also from the location of the site, features of the site, and the surrounding structures in the community. All of this contributes to the design concept of the building, which in essence defines the scope of the project. The architect has covered, at the minimum, the major elements of the work. In a new building project, the schematic design is a set of drawings of the complete building with each area and space within the building designated and identified. The exterior of the building is determined, and usually no further changes to the size of the building are allowed after this phase. In a renovation project, initial design drawings are completed, as they would be in a new building project. These drawings would include any changes to the interior structure—changes in size, number, and kinds of spaces. In addition, these drawings detail the work of improving the various systems of the building.

Changes in the plumbing, electrical, and heating/ventilation/air conditioning systems are also included in the drawings, as are any building additions. The schematic drawings permit the educator to scrutinize the new utility and mechanical systems that will be put into place. Users can determine, for example, whether there is sufficient electrical service to accommodate a projected increase in technology applications in the classrooms. The schematic drawings should be so well defined that any major changes at this stage will not result in additional design fees. The importance of detailed examination and approval of the schematic drawings at this stage cannot be over-emphasized. Failure to do so introduces the possibility of the finished product not fitting the educational program.

Completion of this stage of design represents a milestone for the architect, and the schematic design drawings should be approved by the school board. When approval is given, the architect will have completed approximately 10–15 percent of the total work of the project.

Design Development

Following approval of the schematic drawings, the architectural staff begins the work of developing the drawings that will be used in the construction of the building. The fine points of the design are worked out. During this stage, some of the internal spaces may change form or even size to accommodate the design. The main configuration of the building, however, will not change, unless there are mitigating circumstances. In this stage there should be frequent and continuous review of the work of the architect by school system staff. Not a week should go by without review of the project or parts of the project. The completion of this stage represents approximately 20 percent of the total work of the architectural firm.

Construction Documents

The construction documents consist of a final or complete set of drawings and a set of technical specifications that lists all of the materials used in the construction of the building. This phase represents approximately 40 percent of the total work of the architectural firm. The construction documents are completed by architects, engineers, and technicians who are familiar with the construction materials specified in the design and can describe them in functional terms (Vickery, 1998).

Bidding Advisement

As part of the contract, the architect provides services during the bidding stage of a renovation project. These services can include making an effort to encourage responsible contractors to bid upon the project and evaluating the bids in terms of the budget and the capacity of the bidder. In addition, if the bids are over the budget, the architect will recommend areas in the building where reductions can be made in an effort to bring the project under budget. The architect will recommend that the school staff accept a bid, negotiate with the lowest bidder, or reject all bids. These services represent approximately 5 percent of the total effort of an architect.

Construction Monitoring

After a viable bidder is identified and placed under contract, the architect supervises the project until completed. The supervision entails a periodic review of the status of the project and on-site evaluation of the work of the contractor. The architect must also approve shop drawings, provide material review, and approve all change orders. The architect or a representative of the firm also attends job site meetings. The kind of supervision described above may require a periodic visitation of the site, perhaps on a weekly or bi-weekly basis. If the school system desires daily supervision of the project, the school board should employ a specialist to do that. Having an in-house construction supervisor on the job is a sound investment on the part of the school board. Approximately 20 percent of the total work effort of the architect is expended in this phase of the project.

How the Architect Is Paid

Because school personnel are expending public funds to purchase architectural services, they should expect to get the best possible services available. The best service, however, does not necessarily mean the most expensive services. Obviously, an architect with a worldwide reputation will charge more. In addition, the most expensive architects are usually not the ones who design school renovation projects for a living. This is a further reason why the school system should require previous renovation experience from an architect before employing that person.

Architects normally charge a client a percentage of the construction cost of a building to complete all of the basic services identified above. In some instances, rather than set a percentage of the building cost, architects negotiate a set fee for all of the services, based upon what it costs the firm to produce the size building contemplated. The precise percentage to be charged depends upon many factors, such as the size of the project, the complexity of the building, and whether or not it is new construction. Most often the exact percentage revolves around 6 percent of the total construction cost of the building. In some extreme cases a fee of 10 percent is negotiated, especially for small projects. A school system should normally budget an amount equal to 6 percent of the estimated total cost of the building, for new construction. For renovation projects, the budgeted amount should reflect a higher rate. Seven percent is a baseline.

For services beyond the basic services, such as preplanning, feasibility studies, or extra supervision, a fee is negotiated based upon the salary of the main architect, salaries for other professionals and technicians, materials, expenses, and overhead. This figure is broken down into a per diem factor. The estimated fee is a result of the amount of time needed to complete the work multiplied by the per diem cost.

School and Architect Relationship

The architect is employed by the school board under a contractual relationship. Because of this, the architect eventually answers to the school board and must satisfy its members. The school board can dismiss the architect and void the architect's contract, if they are not satisfied. Payment is prorated up to the dismissal date. Even though the architect is directly responsible to the school board, the actual working relationships are developed with the school staff. The architect and school staff maintain a working relationship by means of frequent interface throughout the entire project. These frequent meetings and review sessions provide the means for design development and eventual approval. In the best situation, regular channels of communication are open between the architect and the staff regarding design issues and effects of the design.

The Best Architectural Services at a Reasonable Price?

Since architects normally work for a percentage of the cost to build a school, prices among architectural firms do not vary too much. Consequently, the cost for a very able architect is the same as for a very inexperienced architect. The secret to obtaining the best possible architectural services is to provide a reasonable fee and promote excellent working conditions for the architect. By this is meant that the architect is provided with clear educational specifications and plenty of staff time to interpret the specifications. This eliminates the frequent changes, which retard the work of the architect.

Architects must work under a set schedule usually dictated by the school system. In order to meet the schedule, the architect needs to have timely input by the school staff, who are called upon to approve completed phases or changes. This requires that the school staff respond to the need an architect has for frequent reviews of the work completed. Therefore, the school staff must be ready to meet when the architect needs such review. All of these go to make up good working conditions for an architect. One further element of good working conditions is the timely processing of requests for payment by the architect. The architect, and eventually the contractor, need payment on schedule in order to meet their own financial obligations to subcontractors. In some instances, delayed payment to the contractor may place the firm in a precarious position with the creditors of the contractor. The school system should do everything within its power to promptly process the payment requests of the architect and contractor to insure speedy completion of the project. A reasonable architectural fee, based upon the size of the project and working conditions that encourage communication, will attract the most able architects.

References

Brubaker, C. W. (1998). *Planning and designing schools.* New York: McGraw-Hill, Inc.

Graves, B. F. (1993). *Schoolways, the planning and design of America's schools.* New York: McGraw-Hill, Inc.

Vickery, R. L. (1998). *Finding the right architect.* Charlottesville, VA: The Thomas Jefferson Center for Educational Design, university of Virginia.

CHAPTER 16

Renovation Funding

Introduction

A LMOST every state disburses funding for programs the state mandates. Typically, the state funds do not cover the entire needs of the locality, and the school board must raise revenue to fund the difference between what the entire program costs and what the state provides. The underlying concept is that the local educational program is a joint effort between the state and the locality, even though education is a state function.

Every state has approved educational program requirements that the local school system must teach in order to receive any kind of financial assistance. These requirements vary by state—from very few requirements to rather elaborate educational program descriptions. Regardless of the number, each local school system is supposed to adhere to the requirements. Normally, state-approved student tests are required as a measure of how well the mandated program is delivered in the school system.

The state financial grant funds the cost of the required program. The amount paid to each local school system is determined by the staff in the state department of education, based upon data from all sections of the state. The costs of employing a qualified teacher, materials and supplies, specialized equipment, and support staff are the foundation of the basic educational grant. Factored into the basic grant are funds for maintaining and operating a facility to house the students and programs. All of this goes into the final determination of how much the local school system receives.

The basic educational grant does not completely cover all the costs of most local programs, because the state grant is normally based upon an average across the state. In some cases, the grant is adjusted for local conditions, such as the limited financial ability of a school system. Even with this adjustment, the funds are usually not sufficient to cover the entire costs of offering the state-mandated program. Local funds must be used to augment the basic educational program, as well as pay for additions to the program. Most local school systems offer an educational program based upon the needs of the students. This means that the educational program offered in the school is more than just what the state requires. The difference between what the state mandates and what is offered locally is funded from local taxes.

Even though maintenance and operations is normally a small percentage of the basic educational grant, the amount is far from sufficient. The local school system must bear almost the entire burden of maintaining the building and keeping it clean. Maintenance and operations are overwhelmingly funded from local taxes.

The same can be said for the funding of renovation projects. A number of states provide financial assistance for renovation projects, and most of these are on a matching basis—with local money contributing considerably to the total cost of the project. Local school systems can fund renovation projects from the operating budget, only if the project is small enough. Almost every renovation project is large enough that capital funding is required. This means the school board must obtain capital funds from the sale of general obligation bonds.

Each project in the capital improvement program must be priced out, in order for the total cost of the CIP to be ascertained. The architect usually develops the precise figures for each project. When an architect is employed to complete a feasibility study for the renovation of an existing building, the school system provides a detailed description of the type of educational program that is desired in the facility. This description is a set of educational specifications. A set of educational specifications contains detailed descriptions of the following:

- description of the community
- number and types of students to be housed
- type of program they need
- types and kinds of spaces needed
- desired relationship between each instructional area
- student and staff support areas
- needed furniture and equipment
- outdoor play and athletic fields

All of the statements in the set of educational specifications spell out what the school staff desire in the renovated facility. The architect is expected to use this document as a guide in designing the renovation. The architect must decide how and where the various segments of the program will fit and still observe the desired relationships.

In doing this, the architect produces the cost figures to renovate the facility. The final costs to complete the project will enter into the considerations of whether or not to renovate. The first consideration in deciding whether to go forward with the renovation is how well the educational program can be accommodated in the renovated facility. Following this, the decision to renovate will be judged against the costs to construct a new facility.

In determining the cost to renovate, the architect needs to be as precise as possible, especially since these costs will be evaluated against other costs. When the capital improvement program is developed, the school system uses budget cost estimates. These are developed by applying standard per square foot costs to the total square footage to be renovated or constructed. In other words, if an existing building contained 120,000 square feet of space and the school system desired to renovate it, a cost for doing that project would be included in the program. In the above example, the school system would obtain an average square foot cost and multiply it by the number of square feet in the facility to be renovated. Square foot costs can be obtained from several sources. In almost every state, the department of education compiles cost figures for all schools constructed in the year. The average square foot costs are then developed and can be used by the local school system. Most architects have access to sources such as the F.W. Dodge Corporation or Means Corporation. These figures can also be used for budgetary purposes. Even though these cost analyses are only approximate, they are sufficiently accurate for planning purposes.

For an actual renovation project that will be presented to the school board for a decision whether or not to renovate, the cost estimates must be much more precise than state or regional averages. In such circumstances, the architect may rely upon a professional cost estimator or use data accumulated by the architect's office staff. Most architects that specialize in designing educational facilities have accumulated a considerable amount of data relative to building costs. Some of the more sophisticated architectural firms have current data on every part of a building. For instance, a firm may have the exact cost to construct a wall that is 10 feet tall and 24 feet wide. Costs for walls in new construction as well as for renovation would be available. If the architect wanted to know how much the same wall would cost with a classroom door in it, the data base could generate such costs. The architect applies this cost figure to a wall in a classroom scheduled for renovation and adds the cost of demolition. Cost figures for every conceivable part of a classroom or building can be generated by such sophisticated databases. Similar databases can be used to contrast specified materials. For example, rapid cost comparisons can be made between the use of terrazzo, vinyl, or carpeted floors. The data in this base are developed from actual construction costs for the school projects the firm has completed. Such costs are calibrated with cost estimates from figures reported to the various agencies and reporting firms. Having these data available permits an architect to provide very accurate and current cost figures. All cost estimates are based upon actual cost histories. To keep these figures current requires considerable staff time to enter data on a periodic basis. Because new data are entered virtually every week, the figures reflect any inflationary trend in the industry. At the same time, some of the more dated information is normally purged from the database. The database should encompass no more than one year to remain current. Comparison between the cost figures from one year to the previous year is also important to provide an estimate of inflation.

Normally in a renovation project, the site is a given, unless the site needs to be expanded. Thus there is need to provide the school system with figures regarding the cost to develop or re-develop the site. Cost databases also exist for the development of playing fields, parking areas, and landscaping. Again, these figures are based upon previous work in similar circumstances. Furniture and equipment for a renovation project also need to be factored into the total cost of the project. These costs can be easily obtained from appropriate furniture and equipment manufacturers. Many manufacturers install their equipment with that cost entered into the total costs. As a result, the cost to re-equip a science laboratory can easily be ascertained with a good deal of certainty as to the final cost.

The cost to upgrade the technology in a renovated building is not that easy to ascertain from historical cost data. For example, the cost to upgrade the wiring system to support current technology is more complicated, due to the unique electrical and phone systems in older structures, as well as the possible need to modify the structure to accommodate wires, cables, and phone/data outlets.

CHAPTER 17

Alternative Funding Plans

Introduction

WITH the national need to upgrade existing school facilities, reduce the enormous backlog of maintenance projects, and accommodate a growing student population, many school systems are in a situation where they cannot finance all their capital needs. In addition, a severe strain on resources has been generated by the large increase in the cost of school facilities. As noted previously, a government report from the mid-1990s has estimated the cost of doing needed upgrades in schools at $112 billion (USGAO, 1996). This amount, which should be adjusted for inflation, represents only what would be needed to place all existing school buildings in satisfactory condition. It does not address the need for new construction. A financial burden of this magnitude can not be borne entirely by local school systems.

The federal government and most state governments enjoyed a growing surplus in revenue as a result of the economic boom during the 1990s. This situation was not true for the local governments, which continued to suffer from a lack of sufficient tax-based sources to meet their needs. Now that the national economy is in financial straits, and many state governments cannot balance their budgets, the situation at the local level has become critical. In case after case, school systems do not have any leeway in going into debt or raising taxes to pay for keeping their buildings in good condition. To remedy this situation, many local school systems and states have tried alternative funding plans.

Popular Funding

Alternative funding sources have become popular. Some very creative ways

151

of using streams of dedicated revenue to leverage debt or other enhancements have been successfully used. In addition, certain models of alternative funding from sources other than school systems have been tried. For example, alternative funding schemes and practices used to implement the Clean Water Act have been suggested for use by school systems.

Caution is necessary in discussing alternative schemes to fund educational capital improvement projects. The first caution is that most alternative funding plans are site-specific. In other words, the alternative funding plan can be used for a specific school building project, but may not be applicable to other school sites in the school system or to school systems in other locations. Moreover, most alternative funding plans cannot raise the entire cost of a single capital improvement project (AGC/AASA, 1996). Many times the funds realized under any alternative funding plan are usually limited. As a result, local funds must be used to augment the funds obtained through alternative sources.

With these qualifications, alternative funding plans applicable to all legally acceptable capital improvement projects should be used to the fullest advantage. Administrators need to be aware of possible plans that may be available in their particular state and locality, because not all plans are universally applicable.

A renovation project for an existing building would in and of itself, probably not qualify for many of the alternative funding schemes, yet under a capital improvement program, funds from alternative funding sources could be used for such projects. Therefore, it is important that such plans and actions be discussed to give the school administrator a better perspective of funding possibilities. Most alternative funding plans address new construction, but building improvements qualify under most definitions of alternative funding. As a result, a renovation project might qualify.

Special Assessment Bonds

A type of debt financing used for school improvements is the special assessment bond. Occasionally, school systems can increase taxes for special purposes such as reducing the deferred maintenance needs. These taxes are a special purpose tax and are usually not considered permanent. The special tax increase may be upon the real estate of the community, upon personal property of the citizens, on operations of commercial firms, or upon other goods or services of the community. Funds generated through this means must be repaid from annual installments from the operational budget.

Non-debt Financing

There are several vehicles for raising funds for capital construction that do not increase the debt of the school system. Some of these vehicles include leasing buildings, public-private partnerships, and special purpose 501(C) 3 Corporations (AGC/AASA, 1996). None of these vehicles generate debt for the school system.

Lease Financing

Leasing of facilities may have several names: installment purchase, installment sales contract, or lease-purchase agreement. Regardless of the name, this vehicle permits the school system to lease a facility by annual payments of a predetermined amount over a period of time. Such an arrangement allows the school system the use of a school building without the initial cost and subsequent debt on its books. Each year the lease payments must be renegotiated, but there is no up front money for the school system to raise. After a period of years, the school system may purchase the facility for a nominal sum. Lease arrangements may even cost less than borrowing the funds to construct the school. The benefits to leasing are no initial funding of the building, steady payments over a set period of time, no incurred debt, and the possibility of purchasing the building at the end of the lease period. The decided financial benefits to leasing might be overshadowed, if the building is not constructed according to the specifications and needs of the school system. The school board should insist the school be built to the specifications the school system has written before entering into any lease agreement.

Under lease agreements, the company that constructed the buildings owns the facilities, and it remains the owner until such time as the school board purchases them or abandons them. Because the facilities are owned by someone other than the school system or local government, the owners must pay local school taxes. In this manner, the school system benefits from not incurring new debt and also from revenue in the form of taxes from the owners. Another benefit is that a lease arrangement does not have to pass a vote of the electorate through a referendum.

Leasing arrangements are a very good vehicle to obtain needed facilities without incurring debt. Private and parochial schools would greatly benefit from lease arrangements. It would be to the benefit of the private and parochial school if a non-profit, tax-exempt organization could construct the building and lease it to the school. In this case, the organization responsible for constructing the facility must undertake the burden of obtaining the financing, while at the same time, the financing agency must bear the risk of lease payments being appropriated by the school board.

Privatization

Public-private partnerships have become more common within the past two decades. The term privatization, in this context, has taken on the meaning that a private company assumes the role of a public agency in the acquisition of a site, obtaining site development approvals, supervising the design and construction process, and managing the public facility when it is completed (AGC/AASA, 1996). The private company may perform any or all of the services necessary, as determined by the school system. Ownership of the facility remains with the private company and at some future pre-determined date, ownership may be transferred to the school system for a nominal payment. As in the leasing arrangement, the building remains on the tax rolls, and the owners must pay real estate taxes to the school system. At the same time, there is no initial outlay of public funds to construct the school. The public-private partnership can capitalize on the strengths of each organization. The private entity can bring savings in construction and maintenance costs that might not be available to the school system, and may circumvent some of the bureaucratic interference associated with public organizations. The private entity may also be more creative in financing construction.

Private and parochial school organizations can also benefit from such partnerships with private concerns. There have been some excellent examples of this approach in funding facilities with both private and parochial schools throughout the country. This example of alternative funding could well serve these kinds of school organizations, which may not have the capacity to float debt on the open market.

Non-profit Corporations

Under specific rules of the Internal Revenue Service, non-profit corporations can be formed to issue tax-exempt bonds for the purpose of developing public facilities. These corporations are known as a Special Purpose 501(C) 3 Non-profit Corporation. This entity is a variation on the public-private partnership. A private entity, such as a business, professional association, or semi-governmental agency can partner with a school system to form a 501 (C) 3 non-profit corporation with representatives from both sides on the board of directors. The non-profit corporation issues tax-exempt bonds and sells them on the open market, through a bonding corporation. The proceeds of the bonds are used to purchase a site, construct, and furnish a school building. The ownership of the school remains with the non-profit corporation, and the school system makes periodic payments to repay the bonds. At the end of the term of the bonded indebtedness, the school system can purchase the school for a nominal fee. By using a 501 (C) 3 corporation, the school system can gain the efficiencies in purchasing and constructing buildings that a private corporation can provide. At the same time, there is no indebtedness occurred by the school system. The school building is planned and designed according to the specifications of the school board.

A non-profit corporation would be an ideal vehicle for private or parochial school organizations to use in trying to renovate an existing building or for construction of a new facility. The same benefits the public schools enjoy through a non-profit corporation accrue to these school organizations. In a school organization with a minimum of support staff, all of the day-to-day work associated with site acquisition, planning, designing, constructing, and furnishing the building would be assumed by the staff of the non-profit corporation. Staff salaries and expenses associated with the administration of the planning process could come from the proceeds of the sale of the tax-exempt bonds.

Alternative funding initiatives that originate from the state or federal government may eventually play a role in assisting local school systems to meet their capital improvement needs. Some of the alternative plans to secure funds by using federal assistance are still problematic, and for a number enabling legislation has yet to be passed.

State Revolving Funds

State revolving funds are an effective mechanism for bringing low-cost financing to meet community needs. These funding mechanisms are also considered loan programs, in that the state lends funds to local school systems to pay for capital improvement projects. The return of principal and interest to the state treasury from the local community, would help to build-up an ever-larger fund balance. Under such plans, the state lends the funds at below market levels with favorable repayment rates. A revolving fund is a loan. Technically it is not a debt that could be counted against the debt limit of the school system.

Several states currently have provisions for a loan program to local school systems. The rate of interest charged by the state is usually low, and the term of the loan may be upwards of 20 years. These are indeed favorable repayment terms. Most states have restrictions on the amount a school system can borrow, and there is usually a backlog of requests for the limited capitalized loan fund. Even with these limitations, state loan funds are very attractive to schools.

There are variations of this method, in that some authorities are suggesting that the Federal Government provide each state with matching grants to capitalize state revolving funds. A state can use this grant to help create an independent revolving loan fund to facilitate loans to local school systems. In either case, the return payments would increase the total capitalization of the state fund and provide an increasing supply of money to lend to local school systems.

State Credit Enhancement Programs

Credit enhancement programs basically use the credit rating of the state rather than that of the local school system to sell bonds. Most local governmental units, such as school districts, have a lower credit rating than the state does. Because of this, the local school system would pay higher interest rates on bonds they issued. Credit substitution programs are normally created through a state constitution provision, legislative statute, or both. This legal basis provides a surety of payment by a state government, and thus enables the local school system to realize a lower percentage rate on their bonds. On the other hand, the programs have the effect of shifting debt from one locality and governmental agency to another-namely, a state government that is already burdened.

One major factor in these programs is that through the legal provisions of enhancement, the state provides a cure for default on the part of a locality. The state in essence pays for any default on the part of the school system. If this happens, the cure for the default may be in the form of withholding state aid from the local school system, or the debt is paid through a state school building fund. Thus, the bondholder is assured that the debt will be paid in a timely fashion. While credit ratings assess the probability of full and timely payment of the debt based on economic, financial, management, and debt factors, credit enhancement plans can also reflect legal provisions of public law that protect from possible default.

The extent of credit enhancement depends upon the exact nature of the state program. In some instances, the state guarantees payment to avoid default by the local school system. In other cases, the responsibility of debt repayment rests with a state aid intercept program that diverts standard education payments from the school system to make debt payments. Both of these methods of payment are a very effective way for school systems to reduce borrowing costs by improving the credit quality of bonds issued with this additional security. At present, 22 states (listed in the Appendix) have some form of credit enhancement program.

Tax Credit Plans

Under a tax credit plan, bondholders are rewarded by allowing tax credits to be applied against possible tax liability the bondholder may have. In the plans that have been suggested, tax credits that can be used against Federal tax liabilities are substituted for the interest bondholders would normally receive from the school systems. One such plan that has been approved by Congress is called the Qualified Zone Academy Bond. There are variations of this plan being proposed.

Qualified Zone Academy Bonds
Under Qualified Zone proposals, state and local governments issue "qualified zone academy bonds" to fund the improvement of eligible public school buildings. An eligible holder of a qualified zone academy bond receives annual Federal income tax credits. These annual credits compensate the holder for lending money and, therefore, are treated like interest payments for Federal tax pur-

poses. The benefit of these bonds is that the school system does not have to pay interest to the bondholders. This would in effect reduce the overall cost of the building. In many cases, the interest payments for any construction project normally exceed the original cost of construction by at least two times. Thus, over a twenty-year period of time, considerable money could be saved.

Under the proposed qualified zone academy bonds, a number of requirements must be met for a bond to be classified for tax credits. The first is that the bond must be issued pursuant to an allocation of bond authority from the state educational agency. Second, at least 95 percent of the bond proceeds must be used for renovation or acquiring equipment at a qualified zone academy. A qualified zone academy is a school that is designed in cooperation with business and is located in an empowerment zone or enterprise community or attended by students at least 35 percent of whom are from low-income families. The third requirement is that private business organizations must have promised to contribute to the qualified zone academy property or services with a value equal to at least 10 percent of the bond proceeds.

Qualified School Modernization Bonds

These bonds are similar to the qualified zone academy bonds in that state and local governmental units can issue qualified school modernization bonds to fund the construction and renovation of school facilities. The holders of the bonds receive Federal income tax credits in lieu of interest payments from the bonds themselves. In turn, school systems do not have to pay interest on these bonds—thereby reducing the total cost of a school building construction project. The credit rate of these bonds is set by the Secretary of the Treasury, and the bonds have a term of only 15 years.

To be classified as a qualified school modernization bond, the issue has to meet three requirements. The first is that the U.S. Department of Education must approve the school construction plan of the state or eligible school system. This plan must be based upon a comprehensive survey of construction needs throughout the state, and there must be a guarantee the proceeds of the bonds will be used for modernization of school buildings. The second requirement is that the local school system must receive an allocation for the bond from the state. The third is that 95 percent of the proceeds must be used for construction or renovation of school facilities. In contrast to the qualified zone academy bonding method, business establishments are not required to contribute goods or services to school systems under this program.

References

Associated General Contractors/American Association of School Administrators. (1996). "Quality of life . . . Investing in our children's future. The case for building maintaining our public schools." Arlington, VA: The Association, ED 436 931.

Council of Infrastructure Financing Authorities. (January, (1998). "State revolving fund: A decade of successful SFR performance, 1987-1997," Washington, DC: The Council.

Drucker, R. D. (1994). "Using impact fees for public schools: The Orange County Experiment," *School Law Bulletin,* Vol. 25,No. 2, pp. 1–14.

Standard and Poor. (1998). "State credit enhancement programs," Tax-backed Debt, New York: Standard and Poor's Municipal Finance Criteria.

United States General Accounting Office. (1996). *School facilities: America's schools reporting differing conditions.* GAO/HEHS-96-103.

CHAPTER 18

Bidding and Contractor Selection

Introduction

BIDDING for any type of procurement of goods or services in the public or governmental sector is a formal and complicated process, bound by legal strictures to insure fairness to all concerned. Competitive bidding is the most equitable way to obtain goods and services for an organization. The procedure is designed to ensure that all qualified contractors and vendors have an equal opportunity to supply goods or services. Failure to use a competitive bidding process is not in the best interest of the school system or the general public, and it may violate ethical and legal regulations. When a formal competitive bidding process is not used, questionable practices can enter into procurement.

There are many misconceptions regarding procurement and how it operates; therefore, everyone connected with this process should be familiar with the prevailing local and state legal requirements governing procurement. Only with a sound legal knowledge of requirements can the persons in the school system responsible for procurement administer the process properly. Every state requires the local school system either to have a procurement policy that embodies sealed or open competitive bidding or to use the policy of the state. If the local school system does not have such a policy, it is usually enjoined to apply the state procurement policy when going on the open market. It is wise for a local school system to have a procurement policy statement in its board policies, to protect it from practices that might be questionable. The school board policies relating to procurement practices should address what goods and services are to be bid and the size of these projects or acquisitions. The policies should also direct school employees in how to apply procurement procedures. Normally, the procedures stipulate which goods and services must be obtained through the bidding process and which may be purchased outside the formal requirements. Usually, a dollar amount is specified as the bottom limit of goods or services that must be obtained through bidding. For goods or services below the set amount, a different means is used for procurement. The dollar limits may be set as low as $10,000 or as high as $25,000. In some school systems, the procurement policy might state that any and all renovation or maintenance projects that the school staff cannot complete are to be bid to outside contractors or vendors. Though it does mean more work on the part of the administrative staff, bidding out is undoubtedly the most efficient procedure for assuring the lowest prices for services.

In addition to the dollar limitation, the procurement policies should also make provision for such matters as advertising, bid openings, pricing, awarding, rejecting, and withdrawal of bids. The policies must also lay out the methods for bonding and qualifying bidders, safeguards that are important for the protection of the school system to assure compliance with all of the regulation of the school board. Precise statements governing each of these topics are necessary to insure that the actions of every employee of the school system are uniform and legal.

Not all bidding is sealed and competitive. The dollar limitation cited above governs what must be bid through the more formal competitive sealed bid procedure. A good deal of material purchased by school system employees does not fall within that limit, and a modified system is used. In many cases, principals of a school building can buy items directly on the open market by a modified bidding procedure. For example, if a principal needs a small quality of pencils or pens, these may be obtained locally through a bid process that insures some competition, but does not use sealed formal bids. In this case, the principal may telephone three vendors and state what is needed. The vendor gives the principal a price on the commodity. The principal then decides which price is the best. There is usually some quality control through the use of descriptors of the product, which could be brand names or some other type of qualification. The decision to purchase is left to the principal, who is expected to know the quality of the product desired. In some cases, the principal may defer to the purchasing department of the school system for help. Often, modified bidding is limited to emergency shortages in a single building, because the school system can obtain better prices when the needs of all buildings in the system are combined and put out for public bid.

Bidding Documents for Renovations

Bidding for renovations and other large-scale architectural projects involves the assembly of extensive documentation. In the final stages of the design process, the architect prepares documents that are called bid documents or contract documents. These consist of a complete set of final architectural drawings and the technical specifications, which are the documents contractors use to develop a price and make a bid. There are at least four sets of drawings each for the various crafts working on a project. One set of drawings is for the structural and mechanical part of the buildings. Another set of drawings details all of the electrical circuits, outlets, and wiring schemes that need to be put into the building. A third set outlines the plumbing and drainage systems required in the building. The final set specifies the heating, ventilation, and air conditioning (HVAC) systems.

The drawings will be used by engineers in the various disciplines to make the plans for the contractor. There may be other sets of architectural drawings, depending on the complexity of the building. For example, there may be separate drawings detailing the communication system. There might also be drawings for special facilities within the building such as the television studio, kitchen, or a stage area. All of these are included in the total package of architectural drawings used for the bid documents.

Architectural drawings can have different names depending on their use. The drawings used in the bidding process are the *final architectural drawings*. The final drawings become the *bid documents* at the point they are issued to a potential bidder. These same drawings become the *contract drawings* when a contract is signed. Subsequently, they become *working drawings* when the contractor uses them during construction. The drawings are all the same, but are used differently during bidding and building. In addition, during the construction phase, shop drawings are developed to detail parts of, or installations in, buildings.

The architect is responsible for preparing and signing all drawings to be used by the school system in the bid process. The architect's registration number and seal are placed on each page of the drawings. In effect the drawings thereby become legal documents, in case of any question as to design or responsibility. The architect also prepares the technical specifications, which describe in detail all of the material to be used in construction—from the mix of the concrete, the size and number of brick or stone needed, to the kind of roof, and even the quality of workmanship. The bids themselves are based upon the contents of the technical specifications.

Every contractor or builder has estimators on staff, whose job it is to help the firm develop a best offer to be submitted to the school board. This is done by pricing-out the material and labor needed to complete the job. These estimates become the basis for the submitted bid. Trying to compete for a contract is arduous and requires the greatest diligence in knowing the future cost and availability of materials. Likewise, a good knowledge of the labor market is essential to making a sound bid, since the largest cost of a building project is labor. Again, the final drawings and a set of technical specifications become the bid documents given to potential bidders.

Pre-Qualification of Bidders

School systems desire potential bidders to be pre-qualified before they submit a bid on a construction project. Pre-qualification means that the school system requires contractors to meet conditions in order to work for the school board. It is a standard way of vetting contractors. The school organization most likely will ask the assistance of counsel in developing the conditions for an RFP. For example, all contractors must post a surety bond before submitting a bid for any kind of work. In a manner of speaking, this is a preliminary pre-qualification, because the contractor must furnish an independent agency with data regarding the firm's financial status. The insurance company that supplies the surety bond to the contractor has investigated the firm to the extent they can report from the data they have that the contracting company is financially stable and there are no current judgments, liens, or legal actions against it. This alone is a very important pre-qualification. However, pre-qualification for a school system normally means something more definitive than a surety bond. Pre-qualification may refer to any demand the school system wishes to make, such as location of the main office, number and types of employees, amount of experience the firm has had with the size of the project being bid, and perhaps a more rigorous scrutiny of the financial standing of the firm than was done by the insurance company.

Some school systems require the firm to employ local workers. The City of Philadelphia developed a pre-qualification based upon the number of minority persons employed by the firm. Firms wishing to do work for the city had to have a certain percentage of minority employees on the payroll and in all positions, before they could submit a bid for work. Firms had to submit a list of employees, with minorities identified, before their bid was accepted for consideration. Firms that did not submit lists of employees could not submit a bid. In this manner, firms were pre-qualified for bid submission. This pre-qualification is legal, because it is in line with civil rights legislation and has been reviewed by the courts previously.

School systems may place any pre-qualification upon potential bidders, as long as the pre-qualification has a relationship to the ability of the bidder to perform work. All firms submitting bids for work with the federal, state, or local governmental agencies must agree before the bid can be submitted to abide by the rules and regulations concerning affirmative action and equal employment opportunities. Agreement to the employment practices as derived from the Civil Rights Act of 1964 and its subsequent revisions can be considered pre-qualification of potential bidders. Almost all bid advertisements now carry the stipulation that successful bidders must agree to these practices and submit evidence of such agreement.

Bidding Procedures

The actual process of conducting bidding is rather straightforward and direct, but it must be carried out in a manner that observes all legal requirements and school board policies. The first requirement is to publicly advertise the project and the request for bids. This must be done in the designated legal newspaper of the community. Most often this is a newspaper with a wide circulation in the local school system. The school board can designate a newspaper as the legal print source of announcements and advertisement of bids based upon the amount of circulation and general readership.

The advertisement must follow prescribed rules for content of the request for bids. The actual newspaper copy should contain the following:

- Complete description of the project
- Location of the project
- When bidding will take place
- Materials necessary to submit a bid
- Where these materials may be obtained and costs
- Cost for obtaining such materials
- Deadline for receiving bids
- The type of bid that will be accepted
- When bids will be opened
- The outcome of the opening of bids
- How a firm can be pre-qualified
- Types of bonds bidder must post
- Legal provisions and regulations bidder must accept
- The person or office to contact for information
- Address of the school board

The advertisement should also specify the kind of bid that will be accepted, such as lump sum, cost plus per centum, or fee basis. Normally all three kinds of bids are legally acceptable to school systems, and the type of project under consideration may well determine the type of bid. The most generally acceptable type of bid is the lump sum basis, but on small projects a cost plus per centum or fee basis is typically used.

School board policies must be observed in the wording of the notification for bids, because this represents a legal action of that body that has financial repercussions for the school system as well as private firms. Legally, the notification is printed in the newspaper for a pre-determined number of days before the closing date. The notification or advertisement of the bid offer is not limited to the legal newspaper of the school system. A wider notification is needed in most cases to obtain sufficient interest in the project. Advertisements are placed with such national organizations as F. W. Dodge and Cost Management Data Group publications. There might also be less formal notifications in some of the trade journals that cater to both architects and contractors. All of these notifications or advertisements are designed to create interest in the project on the part of the local school system. In small school systems or in private or parochial school organizations, advertisement on a wide scale is very desirable for exactly the same reason: creating interest in the project. In some instances, an architect may encourage a contractor to investigate the project with the prospect of submitting a bid.

Bids for major renovation projects are submitted in a sealed envelope and must be accepted and stamped by school system personnel before the stated time of closing. Normally, bids are accepted at 12:00 P.M. on the appointed day of closure until the close of business, which is usually 5:00 P.M., and after that time no bids are accepted. Potential bidders are usually requested to hand deliver the bid, to assure proper submittal to the right person. Bids must be received in the proper office of the school system in order to meet the deadline. Bids sent through the mail and not received in the appropriate office at the proper time are not considered. Indeed, often contractors are making last-minute calculations in the hallway right outside of the submittal offices to be able to meet the closing deadline. Discussions with subcontractors and the firms' executives are the norm before submitting the final bids.

When the deadline for receiving bids arrives, the school system conducts a public opening of all bids. This is done at a time and place in compliance with the bid advertisement and in accordance with school board policy. The bid amount and name of each proposer is read and written in public view. Normally, all of the firms that have submitted a bid are in attendance and can see all of the bids at once. Usually, a representative from the purchasing department or the purchasing officer conducts the meeting and actually opens and records the bids. After all bids are opened, the school system or organization must prepare a recommendation to the school board.

A closed meeting of school system personnel and the architect is held to discuss the bids. The architect offers advice as to the adequacy of the bids and may make a recommendation about which bid to accept. This recommendation is advisory only. That an architect has had experience with the firm submitting a low bid might color the recommendation the architect offers. The school personnel, however, are legally responsible for formulating and submitting a recommendation to the school board at a regularly scheduled meeting. The formal action that the school board may take could be to offer the lowest bidder a contract or to reject all bids. The most common reason for rejection of all bids is that all were over budget, and negotiations failed to produce a bid within the budget.

Lowest Responsible and Responsive Bidder

All governmental bodies have a provision in the procurement policies to accept the offer of the lowest *responsive* and *responsible* bidder. The term "lowest responsive and responsible bidder" is very common in the field of procurement and is used extensively in both governmental and non-governmental circles. Determining the lowest bidder is a fairly easy task. Defining "responsible" and "responsive" is more difficult.

Responsiveness of a bidder can usually be determined if the bid submitted is a competitive offer in terms of the offers made by other firms. In other words, if the bid submitted is within a reasonable range of all other bids, it is competitive, and the bidder can be said to have "responded" to the advertisement. If the bid covers the scope of work needed to complete the project within the projected timelines, it is responsive. Responsiveness can also be determined by the manner in which the potential bidder responds to any communication the school system may send to all firms listed as qualified bidders. Meeting pre-qualifications of the school system is another form of responsiveness. Responsiveness pertains to how a potential bidder may interact with the school system and how reasonable and comprehensive the actual offer is. These criteria may be subjectively defined, but in practice a judgment can readily be made as to how responsive a bidder appears to be.

The "responsible" bidder may be more difficult to determine than the responsive bidder. Responsibility is not always defined quantitatively, although there are certain numerical measures that should help ascertain how responsible the potential bidder is. The first measure that can help determine responsibility is licensure. Every state issues a license to contractors to perform a given type of work. Obtaining a license means the firm has supplied the state with data relative to the financial condition of the firm and a history of their experience and qualifications. Based upon these data, the state licenses the firm.

A second measure of being responsible is the ability of the potential bidder to obtain the necessary bonds. In order to submit a competitive bid, a firm must secure a surety bond guaranteeing the school system that the bid is legitimate, and that if its bid is accepted, the firm will carry through to the end of the project. This bond assures the school system that the firm's offer is in good faith. An insurance company analyzes financial data submitted by the firm to determine credit-worthiness. The insurance company considers the financial picture of the firm and the working relationships the firm has had over the course of its history. The insurance company also researches whether judgments have been applied against the firm, any liens exist, or bankruptcy proceedings have been initiated. Both a surety and subsequently a performance bond must be obtained by the successful bidder. Based upon the evaluation by an independent insurance or credit company, bonds are issued.

All legal and fiscal data must be carefully scrutinized by the school board. Moreover, the board must also examine further criteria. The quality of responsibility may also be evidenced from previous work, e.g., a history of good relationships with other school systems. On the other hand, a history of poor performances and owner dissatisfaction are indicators of non-responsible behavior and should be considered very strongly by the school system. Poor performance indicators may include a larger than average number of contractor-initiated change orders, labor difficulties, cost-overruns on projects, failure to meet project deadlines, and even failure to maintain a clean work site. All of these are indicators that the firm may not be the most responsible bidder, even if it is the most responsive.

The school board has a great deal of latitude in making a judgment as to the responsibility and responsiveness of a bidder. The judgment, however, should be based upon sound data that are available from several sources. Many times the school architect or other school organizations may have these data.

A major misconception is that the lowest bidder is the least qualified to complete the project. There have been instances when a contractor does not perform as well as the school system would like; however, being the lowest bidder does not automatically mean that the contractor is less than the best. In fact, general usage supports the fact that the lowest bidder is the best contractor. A good contractor is one that can make a competitive proposal and complete the project within the approved schedule. The contractor does not do this by saving or skimping on materials or quality. All materials are mandated in the technical specifications, and workmanship is constantly monitored as the project progresses. The competitiveness of the contractor lies in the amount of overhead and profit received from the contract. A good contractor reduces the amount of profit and lowers overhead costs to be competitive. Such a bidder may well be the most responsible and responsive. Competitive bidding can never guarantee that every contractor will perform up to standard, but the chances of a poor contractor being awarded a contract are lowered through competitive bidding. Because the school system is a public entity and is governed by public law, competitive bidding must be used.

Rejection of Bids

Rejection of bids is a legal prerogative of all governmental agencies, including the local school board. The basis for rejection has to fall within the legal reasons for not accepting a bid. It is a misconception that a school board may not reject a bid, once it has been tendered. School boards can reject all bids, if they are above the budgeted amount for the project. Further, a school board may pass over the lowest bid offered and accept another. There are many times when all of the bids received by the school board are for amounts above available funds. In such cases the school board must reject all bids. Most often bids above the budgeted funds result from economic conditions, over which no one has control. In times of severe inflation, governmental and public agencies may not be able to keep up with the increase in prices of building materials and wages in developing a building project. When this occurs, there are only two alternatives open to the school board.

The first is to find additional resources to properly fund the project. This is not a viable alternative for the majority of school systems. In some school systems, the capital funds for the project come from passage of a bond referendum that includes a vote of the citizens in the community. Usually, there is very little leeway in the funding of capital projects covered under a bond referendum. Moving funds from one project to another may not be legally open to the school board, and as a result, the only way to gain additional funds is to eliminate funding for one project, to redistribute funds to another. Although such a move is legal, the consequences are usually negative.

The other alternative open to the school board is to reduce the scope of the project under bid. This can mean a re-design, which will incur additional design fees. Additionally, the form of the re-design may depend upon how much the project came in over budget. Trying to reduce the cost of a renovation project is extremely difficult, since so much of the work is intertwined. Deleting portions of a project cannot be done efficiently. Cost cutting may also take the form substituting less expensive materials. Although such reductions are very common, they can affect the durability of the building over time. Reducing the number of coats of paint on the walls, reducing the quality of the floor tile, substituting less expensive windows, or specifying lesser quality of heating unit are cost-cutting tactics. Reductions of space and substitutions of materials done at this period of time are desperation moves to permit the project to move to the construction phase. Such reductions and substitutions do not benefit from a serious consideration of consequences, because the changes must be made within a very short period of time. Usually a bid submitted to the school board is good for at least 30 days, after which the bidder no longer can guarantee the prices of materials and labor. As a result, the school board and school personnel must make a decision quickly regarding what is to be reduced or substituted.

During the design stage, the architect keeps the school board informed of the cost of the project by periodically making cost estimates of the project. During the last phase of design development, the architect makes a monthly report to the school board about the cost of the project. The reason for this is that any inflationary pressure can be accounted for before completion of the project. Once the budget has been set for the renovation project, it is incumbent upon the architect to stay within that limit. If, however, there are economic circumstances over which the architect has no control, project costs might be increased. At that point, the board might be asked to take actions, such as increasing the funding level for the project or reducing the scope of the project.

Bidding Furniture and Equipment

All non-attached furniture and equipment that will go into the renovated building are bid separately from the actual construction work. Any furniture and equipment that are attached in some manner to the building itself are included in the construction contract. Usually the bidding for this furniture and equipment takes place during the last six months prior to completion of the renovation with delivery directly to the building. In this manner the school system does not have to warehouse the furniture and equipment while the building is being renovated. The F & E budget is usually separate from the construction budget.

Writing the specifications for F & E is the responsibility of the school system staff. Many school systems desire to have all of the furniture and equipment in every school building of a uniform make and therefore specify exactly the kind for each project. In large and medium sized schools, there are purchasing personnel versed in writing such specifications. School personnel also conduct the bidding procedure for these items.

In small school systems, the architect may be employed to write the specifications. This task would be in addition to the design work and require additional fees. Completing the F & E specifications may represent a fee of up to five percent of this budget, but this is a small charge, when one considers the total amount of funds expended for furniture and equipment, and the lack of sufficient staff to do the job inside the school system. The work of writing the specifications can also be contracted out to consultants and even to vendors, although use of the latter may present problems of objectivity. Some school systems release an employee from regular duties to write F&E specifications. There are a few cases when the architect is asked to bid the equipment and furniture with the contract; however, this is not the norm.

Bonding Requirements

When a contractor presents a bid for work to the school system in accordance with the bid advertisement, a surety bond must accompany the official bid. If it does not, the bid is not considered. The surety bond is a good faith guarantee to the school system that the offer is bonafide and that the good will of the firm is behind it. The bond also is recognition that the bidder is ready and able to enter into a contract to do the work. In the unlikely event the bidder is not able to enter into a contract, the surety bond serves as an indemnity for the school system. If such were to happen, the bonding company would pay for any damages this action caused the school system. Surety bonds are usually in the amount of 5–10 percent of the total bid offer and are stipulated in the bid advertisement.

When the school board accepts the offer of a bidder and both parties have signed a contract, the surety bond is returned to the firm. The successful bidder, however, must present to the school board at the time of contract signing a performance bond guaranteeing the work of the firm. The performance bond is in the amount of 100 percent of the contract price. In addition to that bond, the successful bidder must provide bonds covering possible liens from sub-contractors as a result of claims against the firm. These are called performance bonds and held by the school board until the work is completely finished and all settlements are made. This could be from at least 3–5 years following the completion of the building.

The surety bond is a guarantee that the original bid is an earnest offer and that the firm will enter into a contract with the school board. The performance bond on the other hand, guarantees the work of the contractor. There is a big difference, but both kinds of bonds are essential in safeguarding the interests of the school system. The surety bond indicates the price is a firm offer, and the contractor is willing to stand behind it. The performance bond provides some guarantee of the completion of the project with good workmanship and within the schedule.

The performance bond provides guarantees, but some people may believe the bond provides more protection than it actually does. The performance bond does not guarantee that the total price of the construction will be paid to the school system if the contractor fails to complete the project. The performance bond indemnifies the school system only to the extent of losses sustained in not getting the project completed, which could be due to a number of reasons, such as contractor negligence or the demise of a company. In such circumstances, the insurer will assist the school system to obtain a new contractor.

The Contract

After the successful bidder has been identified and recommended to the school board, a resolution is passed by the school board to the effect that the offer is accepted and a contract is to be issued. This is the legal groundwork necessary for the school board to enter into the contract. The contract that is signed is a standard form that is used throughout the industry. Many school systems prepare a specific contract that might include special clauses appropriate to the locality. Nevertheless, all contracts must contain certain wording to express the work to be done. The contract makes direct reference to the bid documents, i.e., the architectural plans and technical specifications. Specifically, the contract states the contractor will construct the building in the manner prescribed, with the type and kinds of materials specified.

The legal counsel for the school system is responsible for drawing up the contract and having the school board execute it with the contractor. That part of the contract dealing with the general conditions stipulates the scope of the project and the schedule. Also in this section are clauses dealing with the payment schedule, the lump sum price, time of commencement, substantial completion, penalty clauses, and final payment. The special-conditions section of the contract states that the contract documents will consist of the agreement, the conditions of the contract, the architectural drawings, technical specifications and all addenda issued prior to, and all modifications issued after, execution of the agreement. Any special conditions that require additional work on the part of the contractor or that the contractor must be aware of are listed in the contract.

In construction contracts, school organizations should address the last 5 percent of the work to be completed. That last little bit of construction work is the most difficult to get completed. If penalties or incentives for completion can be written into the contract, this is an advantage to all concerned. In addition, there should be a stipulation in the contract that any technology or equipment that is part of the contract will include training for personnel.

The contract that is signed by the contractor calls for good quality of work to be performed in the completion of the building. Determining good quality is difficult, but any experienced builder can easily identify the difference between good quality workmanship and poor quality. Upon identification of inferior workmanship, the school representative must document this fact and then let the contractor know the work is not acceptable. The responsibility for correcting inferior workmanship rests with the contractor. The architect stipulates the work to be completed, the type of material to be used, the quality of that material, and even the quality of work. It is up to the owner, however, to determine the quality of the work. A school system should have an employee on board capable of inspecting the work and evaluating the quality of the work performed. This responsibility should not be delegated to anyone else, such as construction managers or outside companies.

Construction Supervision

Someone has to supervise the work of the contractor to insure that the project is being done according to the specifications and the schedule. An employee of the school system can best do this type of daily supervision. For what it costs to employ such a person, the school system can save many times the salary paid that individual. In addition, the school board receives timely reports on the progress of the building. The supervisor also guards against any inferior workmanship by daily evaluating the work of the contractor. The supervisor is the representative of the school system and school board in dealing with the contractor, and decisions made by this person are binding upon both contractor and school board. Having an employee of the school system supervising the work of the contractor serves as a guarantee for the school system.

Construction Management

There are firms that will provide supervision during the construction phase of the project. These firms are called construction managers and serve as a liaison between school board and contractor. Construction management firms will also provide services during the design stage, by offering advice to the school board regarding the type of materials to be used in the project. The services of a construction manager can run from design development to the end of the project, which might include providing the contractor for the work. Such all-inclusive services are similar to the design/build concept, in that an outside management firm controls all of the processes involved in the design and construction of a project.

On first impression, the use of construction management firms seems like an ideal solution for school systems that have limited personnel and little expertise in this line of work. There are many instances where this is the case, but it means the local school system must abrogate some of the supervisory responsibilities to individuals outside of the school system. When decisions regarding the types and kinds of materials and finishes are concerned, the school board has very little input, if they have employed a construction management firm to provide the supervisory services. The substitution of materials and finishes becomes the domain of the construction manager and not the school board. In practice, the school board finds construction management firm personnel make the vast majority of decisions the school staff would normally make regarding these items. The school board would be much better off by employing someone with construction experience to supervise the work of the contractor and to make on-site decisions when necessary.

The cost of the construction management firm may vary from 3 to 6 percent of the cost of construction. This amount is in addition to the 6 percent charged by the architect. That is a considerable amount of money compared with the employment of a supervisor.

If, however, the school board wishes to use a construction management firm to supervise the construction, there are several criteria that should be used to evaluate the firm before signing a contract. These criteria are:

- The background and experience in construction of elementary, middle, or high educational facilities
- A list of satisfied clients that can be contacted for references
- Amount of work of the firm that is repeat business
- A demonstrated track record of on-time and under-budget completion of the project
- A process for preparing and managing the project budget
- A process to ensure effective management of contractors and subcontractors
- Qualifications of the key personnel who will be assigned to this project and their experience on similar projects
- Interaction with, and use of, small, minority-owned, and women-owned businesses
- How will the firm interact with the school staff?
- Will the firm act as a partner of the school system and represent the school board?
- Will the school staff be included in the decision-making process?
- What kind of a fee will the firm charge?

Change Orders

There are times when the specific type of material specified by the architect is not available and a different type must be substituted. For this to take place, there must be a change in the contract under which the contractor is working. As a result, a change order is initiated from the contractor. The architect of record and the school staff must approve all change orders prior to these being presented to the school board for action. If the school board approves the change order, the contract is changed.

A change order literally orders a change in the contents of the master contract under which the contractor is working. A change order often entails changing the amount of funds required to complete the project. The new material may cost more than the originally specified material in the technical specifications. In this case, the cost of the contract is raised accordingly. Change orders can be initiated for a number of legitimate reasons, such as the use of materials and finishes other than the ones called for in the original contract. They can be initiated because the school board does not like the color of the carpeting specified and wants it changed. Change orders can result when the contractor encounters rock formation when digging for the foundations. Such an order would naturally increase the amount of the original contract. Every project has change orders, because no one can anticipate everything.

Change orders can be initiated by the contractor or the school staff. Even an architect can initiate an order for some kind of change when certain site conditions require it. The school system and architect will initiate very few change orders, if they have planned the project well. The number of change orders and the amount of each change initiated by the contractor can sometimes be an index of quality. In most instances, a good contractor will initiate very few change orders. Conversely, a large number of change orders can be a red flag. The frequency of change orders issued in by contractors should be examined by the school during the bidding process.

References

Brubaker, C. W. (1998). *Planning and designing schools.* New York: McGraw-Hill Publishers.

Council of Educational Facility Planners, International. (1991). *Guide for planning educational facilities.* Scottsdale, AZ: The Council.

Vickery, R. L., (1998). *Finding the right architect: A primer for educational design.* Charlottesville, VA: The Thomas Jefferson Center for Educational Design, University of Virginia.

CHAPTER 19

School Operation During a Renovation

Introduction

A LMOST everyone has experienced home renovation. No matter how large or small the project may have been, most likely the normal activities of the household were disrupted. The renovation of a school building presents situations similar to those the householder experiences when a home is renovated. The same displacement of activities from one part of the building to another and then back again occurs, along with the same interruption of a sense of belonging and the forced use of ill-fitting temporary spaces. A renovation project in a school building demands a great deal of perseverance and patience on the part of the administration, faculty, staff, and students.

The benefits of renovation offset the inconveniences. Several research studies provide data demonstrating the advantages of renovating a building. Cramer (1976) studied the effect of renovation upon student attitudes and behavior in junior high schools. The schools were in three classifications: (a) newly renovated buildings, (b) new school buildings, and (c) old dilapidated buildings. An attitude scale was administered to all 2300 students in these buildings to obtain data relative to their feelings. Students in the old buildings scored lower on the attitude scale than students in the other two buildings. Also, students in the old buildings had a higher major disruptive (discipline) incident ratio per pupil than did students in the other two buildings. Maxwell (1999) studied the effects of a renovation project on student achievement in three New York elementary schools. She investigated the relationship between student achievement scores and the building's condition before, during, and after a renovation. Her conclusion was that the actual construction process did have a negative influence upon student performance, but when the renovation project was completed, students performed better on tests than before the project began. Renovation projects also affect the work of the faculty and administration. In a study of a high school undergoing a renovation, Dawson and Parker (1998) questioned teachers and administrators about their work. The conclusion of the researchers was that although the actual renovation caused distress, the end result was better morale, improved working relationships, and deeper pride in the building by the teachers.

The decision to renovate a building does not directly hinge upon the benefits students teachers and administrators derive from the building, but the research findings most certainly should play a part in the final decision. The influence a building has upon student achievement and behavior and teacher performance is well documented and should be a consideration in deciding upon a renovation. Students generally perform better on any academic measure in either a new or newly renovated building, and this should be a strong motivation to school board members to house students in safe and modern facilities. Likewise, teachers can do a better job of teaching when they are in buildings that have all of the amenities associated with a good work environment.

Role of the Principal

When the school board decides to renovate an existing building that is currently housing students, there are many problems to be solved. The key individual in solving these problems is the principal (Futral, 1993). The principal, along with the remainder of the administrative staff, must take a leadership role in helping the teachers, staff, students, and community make it through the project in an orderly and successful fashion. This is not an easy task, but one in which all of the participants, as well as the central office, work together to the greater end. A successful renovation project can foster higher morale and more cooperative working relationships, as evidenced by research findings.

The major role of the principal during a renovation with students in the building is to make certain of the following:

- Interruptions to the educational program are kept to a minimum during the project.
- Students, staff, and school visitors are safe at all times.
- Proper space and equipment are available to the students and teachers when needed.
- School property is secure at all times.
- The school organization is cooperative with the contractor (Earthman & Drager, 2000).

This is a large order for the principal, especially when that person is responsible for the day-to-day activities of supervising the faculty and staff. In some large school systems, the principal may be relieved of direct supervision duties, and an assistant principal takes over the direct supervision activities. In this manner, the principal can devote required time to interface with the building contractor. More often than not, however, school boards do not see the benefit of this arrangement and require the principal to do double duty in being the active educational leader of the school, while also interacting with building contractors and vendors.

Determining the Future Educational Program

The principal must lead the faculty and staff in defining and implementing the educational program to be offered in the renovated structure. This is a formal task, since the educational specifications are needed by the architect in order to design the project. Planning a renovation project, just like planning for a new school, is an opportunity for the faculty and administration to renovate the educational program currently offered. The process of re-examining the curricular offerings and the instructional strategies used is a beneficial exercise. During this process, teachers and administrators can realize the strengths and weaknesses of the existing program. If changes are decided upon, the faculty can begin an investigation of newer methods, materials, and offerings. A re-examination of existing programs may be done with the help of in-house curriculum specialists or outside consultants. The key is the mutual acknowledgement that the physical renewal of the building provides an opportunity for instructional renewal.

Program re-examination employs many different types of exercises, investigations, and visitations to schools where new programs have been implemented. All of these data-gathering and assimilation activities work toward clarifying what the educational program will look like in the renovated building. They should also lead to the development and writing of a set of educational specifications, which will be used by the architect to complete the design development phase of the project. It is the principal, and more specifically, the principal's vision that guides this activity. He or she must have a clear concept of which educational specifications are desirable and workable.

Developing Educational Specifications

Developing a good set of educational specifications is a time-consuming task. Through an analysis of the existing program as described above and a needs assessment of the students and community, sufficient data should be gathered to determine the relevance to students of the current educational offerings. From this process it will be possible to write the set of educational specifications needed for design development by the architect.

In examining the educational program, the faculty and administration should also consider the role of the school in the new information age. Too often, school staff think technology means only computers. The field of technology includes many types of applications of both hardware and software. At one time a chalkboard was new technology, as was the typewriter, and the motion picture projector. The array of machines and programs available to teachers on the open market seems endless, but the real issue is how to use technology for the most beneficial learning by students and effective teaching by teachers. Schools sometime fall behind in having and using the latest technology development, because of the speed in improvement and the cost to purchase new equipment and programs. The schools never have sufficient funds to completely replicate what business firms possess. Through prudent and insightful planning, however, the infrastructure needed for future applications can be included in the present renovation plans, e.g., digitized telephone, video, computer, fire alarm, public address, communication, energy, and other systems. In a renovation project, the school system should consider wireless transmission because of the presence of physical barriers to proper wiring throughout the building, though wireless routers can also be impeded by different types of walls. A successful renovation project should be capable of accommodating the voice, video, and data retrieval and transmission needs of the students and teachers.

Alternative Housing

Renovation logistics are monumental and require the assistance of the most sophisticated planning models. The most common planning tool used by contractors to successfully complete a renovation or any kind of construction project is the Critical Path Method (Earthman, 2000). The CPM is a planning tool that permits the contractor to schedule hundreds of different kinds of activities done simultaneously. The construction activities of the different craftsworkers involved in the building project would quickly grind to a halt without such a planning tool. The Program Evaluation Research Technique (PERT) is another tool used by social scientists for evaluation purposes. PERT is also used to manage large staff efforts, such as a research project. In circumstances where the outcome of a project is not already known, PERT is a useful tool.

In spite of the existence of sophisticated planning tools that enable the administrator to plan a large number of activities at the same time, there are few planning tools available to principals in moving students from one part of the building to another part to accommodate the needs of the contractor. Many times during the renovation project, it is necessary to move students from certain parts of the building, so that crafts- and tradespeople may work in the vacated space. In these circumstances, the big question for the principal is where to put the students. Usually there are never banks of empty classrooms. Nevertheless, there are some alternatives open to the principal to maintain the quality of the educational program and at the same time permit workers to renovate instructional spaces.

Vacant Schools

Some school systems maintain a vacant school building that is primarily used to house a student body when their own building is under renovation. The school system simply moves the entire student body or at least part of it into the vacant building, and the educational program continues with no interruption for as long as the renovation project takes to complete. Not many school systems have a vacant school building standing ready to accommodate a student body whenever the need arises.

Reorganization of Grade Levels

Another alternative is to move students to other buildings in the school system. When a high school is scheduled for a renovation, the lowest grade of that building could be transferred back to the middle school. Likewise, if the middle school is being renovated, the lowest class could be transferred to the elementary school or the highest class could be temporarily moved to the high school. The same arrangement can be applied to the elementary school. In other words, reducing the number of students at the renovation site frees one portion of the building at all times. The remaining students at the renovation site would be rotated throughout the building as the need arises by the contractor. All of this assumes there is space in the receiving school to accommodate the increased enrollment in the school body.

Temporary Classroom Units

The school system can also lease temporary classroom units and place them on the school site. These units can accommodate a class of up to 25 students and be located near enough to the main building to permit students to easily move from temporary classrooms to the main building. The cost of an annual lease is minimal compared with other options and less disruptive to the student body. The downside to temporary classrooms is that the students in these units must travel to the building to use all support facilities, such as restrooms, cafeteria, library, gymnasium, auditorium, and administrative facilities.

Use of Community Spaces

In some circumstances it might be possible to lease space in community facilities to house part or all of the student body. Churches with large educational facilities are good candidates for leasing arrangements. Some museums have educational space that is not used during the day and could be leased to the school system to provide space during the daytime. The Parkway Project in the City of Philadelphia enrolled 500 high school students in a program that used community facilities, such as museums, insurance companies, courts, newspaper offices, libraries, and other available spaces. For a temporary solution, such a proposal would be viable, and the educational experience would be excellent.

Commercial Space Conversion

In some instances, the school system could either lease or purchase vacant commercial buildings for conversion to educational space. Warehouse space that is open and vacant is excellent for such conversion. With the installation of carpeting, temporary walls, suspended ceilings and lighting, the space can become usable educational space for both students and teachers. The cost of conversion would be less than one-third of the cost to find a site and build a new school building. One of the drawbacks here is that usually the warehouses are not located near where students live. Increased costs for security and transportation would be incurred by the school system. Nevertheless, this option is viable when considering the possible costs associated with leaving the students in the building while it is being renovated.

It is also possible to lease office spaces requiring little renovation. No matter which option is chosen, the costs of leasing and moving should be included in the renovation budget.

Safety Precautions

The principal under normal conditions is responsible for the safety and wellbeing of all persons in the school building while school is in session. As such, the principal must institute and enforce health and safety regulations that all individuals must follow. Further, teachers and other staff members must assist in enforcing all rules designed to protect students, staff, and visitors. This very broad responsibility is a serious concern for the principal at all times, because of legal ramifications in administering health and safety policies. The principal is legally responsible for keeping the physical plant free from dangers of all sorts. During the best of times, maintaining good discipline from the students, keeping the building in good order, and eliminating any hazard in the school is quite a task. The task becomes even more daunting during a renovation project. Nonetheless, the responsibility persists, regardless of external circumstances. During a renovation project the principal is responsible for:

- separating the construction area from students
- maintaining good air circulation in the educational setting
- monitoring dangerous construction activities
- maintaining a fire safety system
- maintaining a security system

- ensuring environmental safety (e.g., controlling output of fumes or toxins and controlling the use of propane). (Earthman & Drager, 2000)

These concerns are in addition to the normal concern for the safety of students and teachers. During the renovation certain areas of the building will be blocked off and require different circulation patters for students. Students and teachers must be made aware of such changes before they occur. In addition, these traffic changes may have an impact upon the movement of students with disabilities. The principal must discuss the needs of such students with the contractor before the changes take place.

The principal must negotiate the hours when there will not be any percussive equipment or noisy machinery used near the school building, so as not to interrupt the educational program. The use of propane by the contractor should be closely monitored, to avoid infringement of prevailing fire laws.

The dangers to human safety and life around a construction site are great and need to be emphasized by everyone in the school system. The principal must do every thing possible to insure a separation between the construction site and the students at the school. Severe discipline policies may have to be enacted and enforced to make certain that physical barriers are respected.

Many of these concerns and issues need to be discussed and solved during the weekly job site meeting of the architect, contractor, and school system construction supervisor. The principal should attend these meetings, so as to coordinate the activities of the school and the contractor. Although the principal has no authority over the contractor, any concerns or issues not resolved during the job site meetings should be relayed to the appropriate office of the central administration or to the superintendent in small school systems.

Integrity of the Educational Program

Throughout a renovation, the principal must maintain a viable and continuous educational program. This is not easy if there are constant interruptions resulting from the construction activities. The construction schedule and school schedule should be closely linked to prevent major interruptions of the educational program. The loss of the use of major parts of the building, such as the gymnasium, auditorium, library, or cafeteria due to renovation activities puts a severe strain on the work of the faculty and staff. The contractor must give sufficient notice when these facilities are no longer available to the school.

Perhaps the most crucial facility for the educational program is the library. If renovation work is to be done in that facility the principal must devise an alternative plan so that the functions of the library will continue, even though the space of the library will not be available. A temporary site for the library must be created. It is doubtful that all of the holdings of the library can be accommodated in such temporary facilities, and it may be necessary for part of the holdings to be placed in storage. Selection of the storage area should be done with extreme care, so that books, periodicals, and papers are not damaged by water, humidity, dust or heat. In some extreme cases, the library might have to be dispersed into several classrooms.

Every school has a large inventory of equipment that is used in the educational program. The value of this inventory is very high, both in terms of replacement cost and in loss of use to the educational program. Therefore, the principal must take all due precautions to safeguard this inventory and yet have it available to the faculty and students. This is a very worrisome aspect of renovation for the principal and faculty, and only through due care will the inventory be kept intact. The principal must devise a system of safe storage of all equipment throughout the time of the renovation project. This space would have limited access only by authorized individuals on the staff.

Public Relations

Renovating an existing school building can be a very exciting event in the life of the educational and local community. Renovating a school tells citizens that the school system believes the community is important enough to upgrade the building. A renovation project can serve as the spark to revitalize a neighborhood. Dawson and Parker (1998) recorded the views of teachers and administrators during and after a renovation project. The teachers in this study indicated the process of renovating caused some negative feelings, but once the renovation was completed, faculty and staff morale improved measurably. The teachers felt the administration valued them more, and they were stimulated to deliver better instruction to students.

During a renovation, parents, teachers, students, and central administration needs to be kept informed of the progress of the work. The lines of communication between the school and the above groups should be frequent enough to permit everyone to feel they are a part of the ongoing project. When a section of the building has been completed and students are moved into the newly renovated space, the principal should notify parents of this fact as a kind of milepost. The community should also be notified. Conversely, when something negative happens that might delay the project, or there is an injury on the work site, community members should be told through public announcements of such events. There will be times when the progress of the renovation project may seem to be slowed down for some inexplicable reason. During these times the principal needs to keep up everyone's spirits up by keeping the lines of communication open.

Community Involvement

From the very first discussions to the rededication of the completed structure, parents and community members should be included. Before the actual decision to renovate is made by the school board, there should be community meetings to discuss the possibilities of either renovating the existing building or constructing a new school. The school board and school staff members can actually determine the extent of commitment to the existing building during these meetings. Not every existing school building should be renovated and in those instances, the community should have input before the decision is made. If parents and community members are involved in the process of gathering data and analyzing it, they may be more supportive of the final decision of the school board. If students, teachers, parents, and community members share the same information that the school board has, they will be more likely to favor the decision the school board makes.

There are times, however, when the emotions of community members and parents may be more important than the data presented for consideration. In such cases, the school board and school staff must make a concerted effort to see the possibilities of alternatives other than continued use of an old building for educational programs. By considered involvement of all concerned parties, an agreement can be reached. Consensus may never be reached, but at least sufficient compromises can be made to permit the project to go ahead.

It is possible that community involvement in renovation projects can be leveraged to encourage increased volunteering for the educational program.

Principals can enlist the help of parents and community members in a renovation project to ensure its successful completion.

Below is a list of roles and responsibilities parents and community members can assume during a renovation project. The resourceful principal, however, can suggest additional services specific to the school.

- Attend community informational meetings regarding the scope of the project
- Serve as a representative on the educational specifications committee
- Review the initial architectural drawings and provide input
- Serve on the principal's renovation advisory committee
- Attend a community or school board meeting for a schematic drawing presentation
- Serve as a spokesperson to the school board for school building needs
- Assist in relocating library books when necessary
- Attend periodic informational meetings for community members
- Serve as a community informational leader to nonschool groups

- Help plan for the rededication ceremony
- Serve as a guide/docent for visitors to the renovated building. (Earthman & Drager, 2001)

References

Cramer, R. J. (1976). *Some effects of school building renovations on pupil attitudes and behavior in selected junior high schools.* Unpublished doctoral dissertation, Athens, GA: University of Georgia.

Dawson, C. and Parker, J. R. (1998). *A descriptive analysis of the perspective of Neville High School teachers regarding the school renovation.* New Orleans, LA: Paper presented at Mid-South Educational Research Association, ED 427506.

Earthman, G. I. and Drager, B. (2000). *Experiencing a renovation: A practical guide for principals.* Reston, VA: National Association of Secondary School Principals. p. 44.

Earthman, G. I. (2000). *Planning educational facilities for the next century.* Reston, VA: Association of School Business Officials, International. p. 299.

Futral, K. K. (1993). The principal's role in school renovation. *Principal,* 72 (3): 30–33.

Maxwell, L. (1999). *School building renovation and student performance: One district's experience.* Scottsdale, AZ: Council of Educational Facility Planners, International.

CHAPTER 20

Bringing Closure to the Project

Contractor Notification

WHEN a renovation is finished, the contractor notifies the school board. Officially, this means that the building can be occupied. In cases where students have been in the building during the renovation, the notification can mean that all spaces in the building are now ready for use, even though students may have been occupying some spaces that were renovated earlier. In a new building project, the term "substantial completion" means the building is complete and is ready for use. In a renovation project, substantial completion means the renovation is complete and that all workers and equipment are removed from the site. It also means that both inside the building and around the site, all material and debris have been cleaned up. This notification does not necessarily mean that all the work is complete and that everything is in good working order. The notification by the contractor is an official action of the firm under contract with the school board. Notification has legal consequences for both the school board and the contractor.

Official Inspection

Notification of completion from the contractor triggers a response by the school board. The board is required to make an official visit to the building for verification that indeed the project is completed. The members of the school board, selected school staff members, and the architect constitute the team that officially inspects the school building. A representative of the contracting firm also attends the inspection. Also, the locality's building inspector must be called in to inspect the work and issue a certificate of occupancy.

At the end of the inspection, the school board must decide if the project is in fact completed. If the board is satisfied with what they find, they will officially accept the building as being complete. The school staff and architect provide input into the decision of the school board. The school board must pass a resolution to the effect that the renovation project is complete. This action discharges the contractor from a number of liabilities and responsibilities. In exchange, the school board legally assumes responsibility for the building. If after this action there is an accident on the school site, the responsibility would normally rest with the school board, not the contractor. Before legal acceptance of the building, contractor liability may persist. In a new building project, the contractor has sole responsibility and liability at the site before acceptance by the school board. Following acceptance, the contractor is relieved of such liability.

In a renovation project, if students are still in the school, utility services such as electricity and water are usually provided to the contractor by the school system. In new building projects, this is not the case and the contractor must assume costs of these utilities until the board accepts the building. In unusual circumstances, the contractor may be required to provide utilities separate from the school operation.

Punchlist

In virtually every building project, not everything is in complete working order at the time the contractor notifies the school board of substantial completion. Light switches, light fixture coverings, and plumbing fixtures may be missing. Likewise, the inspection might have identified certain sections of floor tile that do not match, window apparatus that does not operate, sections of the HVAC system that need to be balanced, or doors that do not close properly. All of these items must be taken care of before the final payment is made to the contractor. The contractor begins a list of items that are not complete at the time of inspection. During the inspection, other items are noted and added to the list. Preliminary inspections of the building by the school staff might identify other items. All of these items and work needs are combined into what is called the "punchlist." The school staff is responsible for monitoring completion of the punchlist. Since this punchlist is part of the last 5 percent of the completion of the project, it helps to have incentives in the contract to ensure that the final items are finished. Often, contractors are not as punctual about this portion of the contract, since the dollar amount left in the contract is negligible. One of the strategies of getting the work completed is to have a significant contracted dollar amount withheld until all of the items on the punchlist are complete.

The punchlist is normally completed before the end of one year following acceptance of the building. Sometimes this does not happen, especially when a specified item is difficult to find, and a replacement is not readily available. Nevertheless, the punchlist must be completed before final payment. In some cases, the school board may retain the final payment beyond the one-year usual limit. This is perfectly legal for the school board to do, because the renovation project is not complete until the punchlist is completed.

Orientation Activities

Orienting the faculty, administration, and staff to a renovated building may not be a required activity, as is the case with a new building. Nevertheless, some type of orientation is usually required of all groups, including the students, for proper use of the facility. The type of orientation might depend upon the extent of the renovation project. Usually a complete renovation might also require added space in the building. The added space might be classroom units, laboratories, or specialized instructional areas. Some orientation might be necessary for these areas.

Whatever the orientation activities are, the students should be heavily involved. In fact, the students who have gone through the renovation should have a large part in determining the kinds of activities for the orientation. A re-dedication of the building might be one activity in which all groups can participate. The orientation activities should be directly related to the fact that the building is part of the community and through the renovation has an influence upon the community.

Parents and community members should also participate in the planning and implementing of orientation activities. These activities could serve as a culminating activity for the community. One orientation activity that should take place is an open house for all concerned to visit the newly renovated building. At this time, a re-dedication of the building to the community could take place. The orientation activities serve as the last phase of the project and publicly certify to the community that the long process of renovation is now ended.

Evaluation

Every capital improvement project, whether new construction or a renovation, needs to be evaluated to determine how successful the project was. Evaluation is easy to overlook at this time, because everyone is pleased to have the building renovation completed and the structure in use. However, there are only certain times when data that is pertinent to evaluation is available. Immediately following completion of the project is an excellent time to gather these data, because the shared memory of the process is fresh. Two things need to be evaluated in this situation. First of all, the product of the renovation which is the building itself needs to be evaluated in terms of adequacy to accommodate the type of educational program that will be offered there. This evaluation can take place anytime following completion of the renovation, but probably no later than one year after completion. School personnel who were involved in writing the educational specifications should be involved in the evaluation process. The basis of the evaluation should be the educational specifications document. The evaluators should examine the school building with this document in hand to compare what was written with the end result of the renovation. The basic question in this evaluation is whether or not the architect and contractor produced a facility as described in the educational specifications. The results of this evaluation can provide information for the next renovation project.

The evaluation should also include cost analysis. Typical measurements are square foot cost, cost per pupil, construction time, number and cost of change orders, cost/benefit ratios, and even life-cycle costing. These are the historical cost comparisons. With a renovation project, however, the uniqueness of the project may preclude detailed comparisons with either previous renovation projects in the school system or projects completed in other school systems. Each renovation project is so localized that it is difficult to make accurate comparisons. Nevertheless, internal comparisons of the project can be made to determine costs of selected features specified in the building.

The second part of the evaluation of the renovation project is to determine the success of the process employed to complete the project. Considerable time and effort on the part of many individuals was expended to plan the renovation. This time and effort was given usually outside of the normal working time for both teachers and community members. As such, it is important to find out how these individuals feel about how they were involved and whether they thought it worthwhile. This evaluation should take place immediately after the building is completely occupied, while people can still remember their involvement. To put the evaluation off until later will produce less reliable data. The evaluation should take place while the renovation is still an important event in the lives of those involved.

There is no standard protocol for an evaluation of the process used in planning a renovated building. The school system wants to know if the persons involved in the planning process felt it was worth the effort and did they get the kind of facility they wanted. The simple way to gather these data is by asking questions relative to their judgments on the matter. Participants should be asked if they would want to be involved if another renovation project in their neighborhood took place. This is probably the most important question because it indicates whether they are satisfied with the process and product. Certain demographic data regarding the participants would be helpful to the school board and staff to determine if the composition of the participants represented the community. The survey instrument developed by the school system should cover the entire process of planning the renovation. This would include the initial preparation of the specifications, the feasibility study, the decision-making efforts of the school board, the design development after approval of the project, and the schematic drawings presented to the school board. Data on participation in the planning of orientation activities might also be included to complete every phase of the process.

There has to be a reason for gathering this kind of information, and the question arises as to how it will be used. Evaluating the building/renovation planning process will enable the school organization to assess its effectiveness in managing future planning of large-scale capital improvement projects.

Evaluation Periods

The purpose of any evaluation should determine when and how frequently an evaluation is completed. This holds for evaluation of buildings as well as processes. Obviously, the evaluation of a planning process should happen only once: when the process is completed. After that, the process is history and can be of no further benefit to the school system. Evaluating a process immediately after it is completed cannot be stressed too much.

Evaluation of buildings, however, occurs on a regular basis for specific purposes. In the case of a newly renovated building, evaluations should commence right after completion. This evaluation, as mentioned above, is for the purpose of determining the adequacy of the building according to the educational specification written for the renovation. The effectiveness of the design team and the review team in complying with the intent and requirements of the educational specifications is made here. This evaluation could apprise the school board of the ability of the architectural firm to interpret educational specifications. It could also determine whether or not the architectural firm will have subsequent employment opportunities with the school system.

One year after this evaluation, the building should be evaluated to determine how well it is holding up to the normal wear of use. Some authorities suggest this evaluation be conducted 11 months after the final school board inspection and acceptance of the building. The reason for this is that one-year warranties of much of the equipment and machinery are still in force. Any excessive wear on the machinery or failure of equipment could be detected before the warranty has expired, and the manufacturer could make proper adjustments.

Following the one-year evaluation, the building should be scheduled for periodic evaluations according to the normal schedule of the school system. Some school systems have a schedule of building evaluation that occurs on a more frequent basis. There is usually an annual evaluation conducted by the principal of the school and the custodian. This evaluation identifies work items that are added to the maintenance schedule for completion according to a timetable.

In a number of systems, central administration staff makes an inspection of the building every five years. This inspection is thorough and includes an appraisal of the machinery and equipment, in addition to the infrastructure of the building. Annual and five-year inspections are performed until the 20th year of use in the building. At this point, a substantial evaluation takes place with the thought of completing a renovation project to bring the building up to standard. Prudent administration would suggest an evaluation schedule such as this, to guard the investment of the community in school buildings.

References

Earthman, G. I. (1994). *School renovation handbook: Investment in America.* Lancaster, PA: Technomics Publishers, Inc.

Hocomb, J. H. (1995). *A guide to the planning of educational facilities.* Lanham, MD: University Press of America.

CHAPTER 21

The Price of a Good Education

Introduction

How much does a good education cost a family or taxpayer? There are many ways to answer that question, and all depend upon how a good education is defined. In purely financial terms, one simply has to multiply the annual cost per student times 12. Every school system in the country has a definition of what constitutes a good education. From this definition evolves the total educational program that is offered in the schools. Most of this definition, in the form of the identified educational program, constitutes what a student is expected to learn either each year or at the termination of school attendance. The educational program is the substance of what is to be learned, but there is more that needs to be in place for a good education than just having an appropriate curriculum. It is understood that the educational program must be implemented and conducted by a good teaching faculty and administrative support staff. In addition, the teachers must have the proper tools to teach and this means sufficient and appropriate books, curricular materials, and instructional supplies to work effectively.

The melding of the curriculum with the instructional personnel and proper tools cannot operate in a vacuum; there must be a place where the student meets the teacher for the educative process to function. This place is normally a classroom within a school building. A building is needed for the educative process to take place. The school building is the appropriate place where students and teachers can meet to learn. Indeed, the building itself protects the students and faculty and nourishes the educational processes that occur within it. The building in which students and teachers are located is part of the cost of a good education. In fact, a good building can be a very costly part of the price for a good education. On the other hand, a poor building can be even a more costly price to pay for an education that is not as good as it could be in a good building.

There is little doubt that the school building influences the performance and behavior of students and teachers. Almost everyone agrees that the physical environment has an influence upon how humans behave, work, and play. This is especially true for youngsters who spend from 6–7 hours a day for 180 to 210 days per year in one facility.

In spite of the fact that almost everyone believes in the building influence, the degree of importance this influence has upon students has been disputed. Recent studies, however, have built a sound foundation of research results indicating the building does in fact account for up to 5 percent and as much as 11–17 percent of the variance that explains student achievement (Earthman & Lemasters, 1996). The findings in these studies have been consistent in the amount of influence the physical environment exerts on student achievement. A recent study in two large urban areas found the difference in student scores to be within the range of previous studies (Schneider, 2000).

How the building influences learning is of immense importance to decisionmakers in the school systems throughout the country. If the building itself has a positive effect upon how well students learn, then a proper facility and physical environment becomes a requirement for all students to successfully learn. In other words, to receive a good education, students need to be in buildings that will promote effective learning and not detract from achievement. The cost of such a building is included in the cost of a good education. Sufficient funds must be available to provide such buildings. School boards must provide the funds for proper physical environments. In this regard, there are two main concerns.

The first concern deals with having the proper spaces, furniture, and equipment to carry on the educational program and to have them in sufficient quantity and in the right location. The educational program requires certain types and kinds of spaces in order for the teacher to carry out the activities needed to teach students and for the students to do those things necessary for them to learn. It is not enough to have sufficient classrooms to house the student population, but specialized learning and support spaces are also needed for instruction in certain disciplines. The instructional methodologies used in a school building also dictate the need for certain physical features and components. In renovation projects, attention needs to be given to how the instructional methodology will influence what is actually done in the building.

The second concern is the influence of the building's physical condition on student learning. The lack of proper maintenance practices can allow a building to gradually deteriorate, which in turn adversely influences student performance.

Educational Program Effect

Educational programs govern the types of space needed

The types and kinds of instructional spaces in a school depend upon the type of educational program and the number of students to be served. For instance, a strictly academic program will require more general-purpose classrooms, lecture rooms, and individual study areas than will a comprehensive educational program. The latter will require, in addition to general-purpose classrooms, various laboratories, shops, and instructional spaces where students participate in hands-on learning activities. These types of specialized instructional areas will augment the general-purpose classrooms. Even the types of specialized instructional/learning spaces will vary according to the needs of the educational program. The specialized instructional/learning spaces require specific equipment and materials depending upon what is taught there. Many specialized instructional/learning spaces demand large areas to accommodate the equipment that is housed there. The size of specialized spaces has increased over the years, so that a science laboratory, for example, is much larger than one that was designed a decade or more ago.

Given that each school will have a variety of general-purpose classrooms and specialized instructic\nal/learning spaces to accommodate the educational program, the mix of spaces will vary according to the student body that is served and the needs of the community. The specification of building spaces stems from a careful analysis of the educational program. Such an analysis is especially critical when planning a renovation.

In addition to the kinds and number of instructional/learning spaces, the location of these spaces will need to be made. Certain relationships between educational places make sense in light of the curriculum. These relationships are important for the efficient functioning of the teaching staff and for the effective learning of students. An example is locating the humanities classrooms near the media/library center, given that the humanities curriculum demands frequent library research. Other such relationships might involve the placement of the little theatre next to the commons area and to the cafeteria.

Specific Program Effects

Classrooms

In a discussion paper on classrooms published by the National Clearinghouse for Educational Facilities in the year 2000, a professor was quoted as saying that classrooms should not be built in a school. Instead, personal workstations for each student should be provided. This is not too far from the suggestion of Alvin Toffler (1980) who wrote some twenty-three years ago that school buildings as we know them might be obsolete. People who advocate abandoning the classroom or the school building indicate their lack of experience in the public schools and their limited knowledge of the social and educational development of children. Classrooms or some aspect of the classroom will always be in the school building, but the exact shape or configuration of the classroom space may well change over the years. Nevertheless, until public education's fundamental tenet of educating all children changes, schools will continue to need classrooms. There must be some kind of space for young students to call home and that is not an independent workstation. Students may well be assigned a workstation for many activities, but there will always be the socialization aspect of a group of students together in one space, such as a classroom.

The question concerning classrooms in a renovation project is how to provide sufficient space for the type of activity that will take place there. Classrooms for elementary students need sufficient space for an activity-based curriculum. This type of curriculum is also offered in middle schools, where larger classrooms are needed. Classrooms in a middle school should approximate those needed for an upper elementary school class, because of the curricular demands. State rules and policies govern the amount of minimum space that should be in a classroom, but school systems can exceed these minimums to provide the kind of space needed for a modern curriculum. In addition, with the introduction of technology, the size of the regular classroom needs to be increased a minimum of 15 percent of the floor space to accommodate this function. One computer takes the space equivalent to that needed for one student. Therefore, either the capacity of the classroom must be reduced for every computer, or the size of the classroom must be increased for each computer. This is difficult to accomplish in an older building, and in many cases the capacity of the classrooms and the total building must be reduced to permit the introduction of computers and other technology.

Compromises on the amount of classroom space for the number of students assigned should not be permitted, because student achievement can be negatively affected.

Science Laboratories

Traditionally the high school science curriculum called for offerings in biology, chemistry, and physics, with each discipline having a different kind of laboratory. The most recent trend is to provide a general laboratory in which all three of the disciplines can be taught. The traditional approach to teaching these disciplines separately is being revised, so that there is a more seamless curriculum for the sciences, which includes all of the subject matter in these disciplines. Whether or not this type of multi-purpose laboratory is what the faculty needs or wants is for local determination.

Physical Education and Wellness Spaces

The most impressive fact about the spaces that accommodate the Physical Education program is that the number and size of these spaces have increased measurably over the past decade. The Physical Education and Wellness programs command a larger percentage of space in the building than previousl y. The increase has been from 15 percent of the total building space in 1970 to approximately 25 percentage of the total space of the building. This speaks to the change in the educational program offered in the school, and to the increase in awareness of the general population in health. A high school built in 1950 might have one gymnasium, two locker rooms, and a wrestling room, plus some small auxiliary spaces to adequately hold the Physical Education program. A high school built today requires two standardized gymnasiums, one with seating for at least 1500-2000 spectators. In addition, the two gyms are supported by three to four locker/shower rooms, training rooms, wrestling room, one or more exercise rooms, and perhaps a weight training room. This is in addition to all of the outside play spaces and tennis courts. All of this adds up to at least 25 percent of the total building space, which is a sizeable increase over prevIous years.

In addition, new laws require equality of physical education space for both genders.

In renovating a high school building that is over 15 years old, many of these physical education facilities can be supplied only by an addition to the existing building. Placement of the new facilities can present a severe problem for the architect in terms of establishing desirable relationships among the various components.

Teacher Office/Work Space

School systems have become aware of the professional needs of the teacher in preparing for the daily teaching assignment, completing certain administrative work, and in meeting with colleagues and parents. As such, most school systems now provide space for teachers to work, plan, and meet. These spaces may be called offices, workspaces, or conference rooms. Regardless of the nomenclature, spaces to accommodate these professional activities of the teaching staff are a necessity. To accomplish this in an existing building is a difficult, but not impossible, task for the planners and design professionals. Traditionally, a high school teacher was assigned to a classroom and stayed in that room every period. The planning period of the teacher was in the classroom. If teachers have a professional workspace, they will not need to use a classroom for preparation and meetings. As a result, a class can be assigned to the classroom for that period. In this manner, greater utilization of all classrooms will result, and at the same time the teachers will have a professional space in which to work.

Community Space

More and more school systems are building spaces in new schools that can be used by the community without interrupting the daily educational program or inconveniencing the teachers or students. These spaces may be meeting rooms, conference rooms, activity areas, or kitchenettes, and are normally in addition to all of the spaces needed by the school program. Likewise, most school systems are building regulation-sized gymnasiums in all new schools, even elementary schools. Normally, the elementary physical education program requires only about 3000 square feet of space as against 10,000–15,000 square feet for a regulation-sized gymnasium. The reason for placing a gym in elementary schools is for the community to use the gym during off-hours and to house any after school activities of the student population. A gymnasium can prove very useful for many community activities besides physical activities.

Computers—Laptops or Labs

Until recently, the standard approach to providing students with access to computers was for each classroom to have 3-4 computers enabling students to do some independent study or enhancement activities. Actual instruction in keyboarding and computer program techniques was done in a computer laboratory with 25–30 individual computers. This arrangement provided for the needs of students in acquiring computer skills and learning through independent study.

With the widespread availability of laptop computers to the general public, some educators have changed their minds about how computer access in school should be done. Some school systems have begun to issue laptop computers to all students. The theory behind this action is that all students would have access to a computer regardless of the financial means of the family. In addition, all students would have the same kind of computer, which facilitates the use of software. Not all school systems can afford to implement such a practice, but this may be a harbinger of what will be commonplace in the future, and educators should plan accordingly for such an increase in availability and use of laptop computers in the schools by students. General use of laptop computers by all students in a school building requires more than just the laptop itself. Students need to have computer ports to access stored data to use in their work. In renovating an existing building, consideration should be given to the need for computer data ports throughout the school building and especially in areas where students can informally use the laptop computer to access information sources. There is no specified number of data ports needed in a situation where laptop computers are available and used, but if a school administration issues laptop computers to every student, a large number of data ports will be required to fulfill the need of every student. In an existing building, especially one that is more than a decade old, consideration should be given to the use of wireless applications for access to data. Wireless networks are extensions of cabled networks and act in the same manner; the only difference is that the computer does not need a data port for input. Wireless applications eliminate the need for laying hard wire throughout the school building. Any classroom or area with an Ethernet drop can become a virtual computer laboratory through a wireless network. These applications are much easier to implement in existing buildings.

The foregoing building trends show that changes in school structures result from curricular mandates, educational technology, and outreach of the school towards the larger community.

The Price to Pay

All of these changes come at a price that must be met by the local school board, since to not meet these educational program needs is to forfeit or compromise the educational opportunities of students. These are the types of spaces the new educational programs of the future will need.

Building Condition Effects

Age of Building

Researchers have investigated the relationship between the physical environment of the school building and student learning. There have been many different approaches to such studies. All of the researchers have endeavored to identify the degree of influence that a building has upon students and teachers. To do this, researchers must identify the variables that might influence students in their learning. The usual method of doing this is to statistically compare student achievement results with the variable under investigation. In the case of the school building, researchers have used the condition or age of the building as the variable to compare with student achievement. Some of the most promising research efforts have dealt with the age of the building and with the assessed condition of the building.

McGuffey (1982) in a review of research cited seven studies that used the age of the building as a variable to correlate with student achievement scores. He reported that all seven of the researchers found significant relationships between age of building and student achievement. Lemasters (1997) in a later review identified additional studies that used the same methodology as the previous set of studies. In all cases, the building age was significant as a contributor to student achievement and behavior. Minor differences in significance were noted on selected grade levels and subjects.

To explore the possible relationship of building age and student achievement, Bowers and Burkett investigated the differences in student achievement, health, attendance, and behavior between two groups of students in different physical environments (July/August, 1988). Two elementary school buildings, containing students between the ages of 5 to 13 years, in the same school jurisdiction in rural Tennessee were used to differentiate physical environments for this comparison. One school was recently opened and was a modern building in all respects. The other building was constructed in 1939 and had very little improvement to the physical structure. The researchers reasoned that the students and faculty in both buildings were essentially the same. The educational program and teacher competency were equal.

The researchers began the study with the hypothesis that achievement and selfconcept of students would be improved significantly in modern school buildings.

Two hundred eighty randomly selected fourth and sixth grade students in two facilities were the subjects of the study. The administrators, teachers, and socioeconomic levels of the communities were similar. The variable of age of the facility was the only difference when comparing the achievement and self-concept of the students.

Students in the modern building scored significantly higher in reading, listening, language, and arithmetic than did students in the older facility. The significance was greater than the .01 level. Discipline was needed less frequently in the new facility versus the older physical environment. This was true, even though the new school had a larger enrollment. The level of significance for analysis purposes was .01. Students in the newer building had significantly higher attendance records and seemed to have better health records. Self-concepts of the students in the newer facility were better than the self-concept of those of students in the older school. Bowers and Burkett inferred that a significant difference existed between students at the two elementary schools in regard to the relationship of the physical environment and student achievement.

Students in the new school building significantly outperformed the students in the older building in reading, listening, language, and arithmetic. Further, faculty in the new building reported fewer disciplinary incidents and health conditions than faculty in the old building. Attendance likewise was better with those students in the new building than in the old school. Bowers and Burkett concluded that a relationship did exist between the physical environment and student achievement, health, attendance, and behavior.

In a study of the relationship between building age and student achievement, Phillips (1997) found significant differences in the reading and arithmetic scores between upper elementary students in new buildings compared with students in old buildings in the state of Georgia. This was a replication of an earlier study completed by Plumley (1978). Phillips found a definite relationship between the age of the school facility and student reading achievement scores as measured by the Iowa Test of Basic Skills (ITBS) and a strong relationship between student mathematics achievement scores and building age. The mean mathematics scores for the treatment group (those students in new buildings) increased 7.63

percentile ranks after moving into the new facility. Phillips' study supported the findings and conclusion of previous studies using age as an independent variable. He did not find any significant differences in attendance patterns between the students enrolled in the old or new building.

Building age can also serve as a surrogate for a number of specific variables such as condition of the building, thermal control, proper lighting, acoustical control, support facilities, condition of laboratories, aesthetic condition of the environment, just to name a few. Many studies have combined all of these factors into one assessment instrument that produces a quality of the condition of the building that can subsequently be compared to student achievement.

Building Condition

Over the past sixty years, considerable research has taken place in the United States to assess the possible relationship between student performance and the built environment. Researchers have mounted studies to investigate the influence of various building components such as wall color, building configuration, the presence or absence of windows in classrooms, air-conditioning, space allocation per pupil, use of carpeting on the floor, noise levels, thermal conditions, and furniture types upon student performance in an effort to discover a relationship. For the most part, these research efforts have proven valuable to the designers of new school buildings. Most new school buildings in the United States incorporate many of the aforementioned elements, because of the research efforts.

The main emphasis of investigation in this type of research is the relationship between the built environment and at least two student variables. The first variable is student achievement as measured by some form of standardized or normed test or examination administered to all students in the schools. The other variable is student behavior, which can denote student activity or school climate. These two variables relate directly to students themselves. There is a common belief among educators that the behavior of students influences their academic achievement. The reverse of this relationship is also believed to be true.

In one of the earlier research efforts to document a possible relationship between student achievement and school building condition, Cash (1993) investigated small rural high schools. She developed a building evaluation instrument to be used by local school personnel to determine the classification of the building. This instrument was based upon existing research studies that addressed certain building conditions. Each item on the instrument was derived from previous studies that had been completed and which showed a positive relationship between a particular building condition and student achievement and behavior. The items in the Commonwealth Assessment of Physical Environment (CAPE) addressed such conditions as: air conditioning, classroom illumination, temperature control, classroom color, graffiti, science equipment and utilities, paint schedules, roof adequacy, classroom windows, floor type, building age, supporting facilities, condition of school grounds, and furniture condition. Each of these conditions has been shown by previous research to be related to student achievement and behavior. The presence or absence of these factors determined the overall condition of the building. School buildings were classified as substandard, standard, and above-standard through a self-evaluation.

Cash compared the mean achievement scores of students in substandard and above-standard buildings to determine if a difference existed between the scores. Cash found that there were significant differences between the scores. She concluded that the condition of the school building did in fact influence student achievement scores. Students in substandard buildings scored lower than students in above-standard buildings. The difference in percentile scores amounted to between 3 to 9 percentile rank scores.

Her study was followed by two other research efforts, Earthman, Cash, and Van Berkum (1995) and Hines (1996). Earthman et al involved a statewide study of all high schools in North Dakota. These researchers found almost exactly the same results as did Cash. Hines used a population of large urban high schools. His findings were outstanding, in that some of the differences between scores amounted to 14, 17, and 19 percentile rank points. In other words, the students in the above-standard schools scored almost 15–20 percent higher than students in substandard buildings. These studies were basically replications of the original Cash study. In both cases, the results were the same with students in substandard buildings scoring significantly lower than students in above standard buildings.

Analyses of data in these studies would indicate that all three studies found a difference in the percentile rank scores of students in the various buildings. In each case the differences were positive. Further, the findings in these studies corroborate the findings in previous studies. Specifically, the findings indicate that in four main subjects of the curriculum of the public schools, reading, mathematics, language/writing, and science, there is a difference in student performance depending upon the condition of the school building. A recent study (Schneider, 2000) corroborates the findings of these studies within the same range of differences. Researchers have new completed these kinds of collaborative studies in four different states and in two large urban cities. The results of these studies represent a sizeable corpus of evidence for the belief that buildings strongly influence student achievement.

The Price of Poor School Buildings

The results of all of the studies cited in this chapter can be played out in possible actions of school authorities and governing board members to improve the educational opportunities of students. If, as the studies strongly indicate, the test scores of students in above-standard school buildings are above the scores of students in substandard building by as much as 1–17 percentile points, then there are ways of increasing student performance and subsequent test scores by improving the condition of the building.

Spending funds to improve the built environment might produce greater student performance results than funds spent on instructional materials, textbooks, and even teachers. The results of these studies at least strongly suggest this proposition.

It has been demonstrated time and again that better prepared graduates of the local school system are more productive citizens. Better-prepared graduates have more productive jobs throughout their lives and in turn are happier. Of course, the corollary to this is that more productive citizens add to the prosperity of the state and support it more evenly through taxes. Consequently, anything that can be done to positively raise the level of achievement of students who will be future citizens, will greatly influence the economy over time.

A confounding dimension to these studies, however, is the long-term influence a poor building may have upon students (Earthman, November, 1998). The longitudinal influence of a *substandard* physical environment could be a very important consideration. If students are housed in poor buildings for a number of years, will the effect on achievement be multiplied? Moreover, will the values of the students be impaired? After long exposure to poor or marginal buildings, will students believe such conditions are normal? It is very difficult to conduct longitudinal research studies on the influence of a building. As a result, we can not with any degree of certainty describe the exact results of this phenomenon in every situation. The research cited here is simply a photograph of conditions and relationships at one time, not over successive periods of time. There may be a cumulative effect of the disparity in student test scores between poor and good school buildings that continues during the time the student is in school.

References

Bowers, J. H. and Burkett, C. W. (1988, July–August). Physical environment influences related to student achievement, health, attendance, and behavior. *CEFP Journal.*

Cash, Carol S. (1993). *School building condition and student achievement.* Blacksburg, VA: Unpublished doctoral dissertation, Virginia Polytechnic Institute and State University.

Earthman, Glen I., Cash, C. S., and Van Berkum, Denny. (1996). A statewide study of school building condition and student achievement and behavior. *Journal of School Business Management;* Vol. 8, No.3.

Earthman, G. I. and Lemasters, L. K., (1996, October). *Review of research on the relationship between school buildings, student achievement, and student behavior.* Paper presented at the annual meeting of the Council of Educational Planners, International, Tarpon Springs, Florida.

Earthman, G. I. (1998, November). *The impact of school building conditions on student achieve-*

ment and behavior. Paper presented at the international conference, The Appraisal of Educational Investment, Luxembourg: European Investment Bank and Organization for Economic Cooperation and Development.

Hines, E. W. (1996). *Building condition and student achievement and behavior.* Blacksburg, V A: Unpublished doctoral dissertation, Virginia Polytechnic Institute & State University.

Lemasters, L. K. (1997). *A synthesis of studies pertaining to facilities, student achievement, and student behavior.* Blacksburg, V A: Unpublished doctoral dissertation, Virginia Polytechnic Institute & State University.

McGuffey, C. W. (1982). Facilities. Chapter 10, in W. Herbert (ED), *Improving educational standards and productivity* (pp. 237–288). Berkley, CA: McCutchan Publishing Corp.

National Clearinghouse for Educational Facilities. (2000, July). *Classrooms.* Don Butin. Washington, D.C.

Phillips, R.W., (1997). *Educational facility age and the academic achievement and attendance of upper elementary school students.* Athens, GA: Unpublished doctoral dissertation, university of Georgia.

Plumley, J. P. Jr., (1978). *The impact of school building age on the academic achievement of pupils from selected schools in the State of Georgia.* Athens, GA: Unpublished doctoral dissertation, University of Georgia.

Schneider, M (2000). *Public school facilities and teaching: Washington, DC and Chicago.* Stony Brook, NY: State University of New York.

Toffler, A. (1987). *The third wave.* New York, New York: Morrow Publishers.

Appendix A

Maintenance Reserve Fund Formula

1. Annual Reserve Fund Needs for Repair of Buildings

$$\frac{\$1,986,534,00}{\substack{\text{Replacement Value} \\ \text{for All Buildings}}} \times \frac{.018 \ (1.8 \ \text{percent})}{\substack{\text{Percent of} \\ \text{Replacement Costs}}} = \frac{\$3,575,761}{\substack{\text{Annual Reserve} \\ \text{Fund Contribution}}}$$

2. Annual Reserve Fund Needs for Repair of Equipment

   Equipment values average 11 percent of building costs. Repair of equipment averages 5 percent of replacement value of equipment.

$$\frac{\$1,986,534,00}{\substack{\text{Replacement Value} \\ \text{for All Buildings}}} \times \frac{.011 \ (1.1 \ \text{percent})}{\substack{\text{Percent of} \\ \text{Building Costs}}} = \frac{\$2,185,187}{\substack{\text{Equipment} \\ \text{Replacement Value}}}$$

$$\frac{\$2,185,187}{\substack{\text{Equipment} \\ \text{Replacement Value}}} \times \frac{.05 \ (5 \ \text{percent})}{\substack{\text{Percent Equipment} \\ \text{Replacement Costs}}} = \frac{\$109,259}{\substack{\text{Annual} \\ \text{Budgeted Amount}}}$$

3. An nual Reserve Fud Needs for Equipment Replacement

   An annual expenditure of 3.33 percent of equipment value means an average life of 30 years for all equipment.

$$\frac{\$2,185,187}{\substack{\text{Equipment} \\ \text{Replacement Value}}} \times 3.33 \ \text{percent} = \frac{\$7,276}{\substack{\text{Annual} \\ \text{Budgeted Amount}}}$$

4. Annual Reserve Fund Needs for Grounds Upkeep

Total square feet of all buildings = _____ Cost per square foot _____
For repair of buildings

5 percent of the square foot cost = _____ Cost per square foot for_____
for repair of buildings   upkeep of grounds

Total square foot of grounds   = _____ Annual reserve needed _____
multiplied by th ecost per square   for upkeep of grounds
foot for upkeep of grounds

5. Annual Reserve Fund Needed

Repair of Buildings $_____
Repair of Equipment $_____
Replacement of Equipment $_____
Upkeep of Grounds $_____
Total annual Reserve Fund Needed $_____

Appendix B

States that Have a Credit Enhancement Plan

California	Eligible city and county bonds
Colorado	Local school bonds
Georgia	Eligible local school bonds
Indiana	Local school bonds, leases
Kentucky	Local school bonds, leases
Michigan	Qualified local school bonds
Minnesota	Eligible local school bonds
Mississippi	Eligible local school bonds
Missouri	Eligible local school bonds
Nevada	Eligible local school bonds
New Jersey	Local school bonds
New York	Local school bonds
Ohio	Eligible local school bonds
Oklahoma	Eligible local school bonds
Pennsylvania	Local school bonds
South Carolina	Local school bonds
South Dakota	Local school bonds
Texas	Approved local school bonds
Utah	Qualified local school bonds
Virginia	All local General Obligation debt
West Virginia	All local General Obligation debt
Wyoming	Eligible local school bond

Appendix C

Maintenance Work Forms

Maintenance Department
Maintenance Request
Request Data

Facility/Location: _____ Date: _____

Description of Request: _____

_____

_____

_____

_____

_____

_____

I verify this is not a duplicate submission or service call duplication.   Administrator's Signature

Phone Number

Response Data

Approved: Yes No Priority: 1 Emergency 2 Urgent 3 Rush 4 Routine 5 Scheduled PM 6 Next Break

Category: Safety   Repair   Maint   Renovate   Remodel   Construction   Warranty   Self Help

Assign to: CARP   LOCK   BLOK   ELEC   FSMC   HVAC   WSHT   PLBR

         LOGS   AUTO   EQMC   EQOP   MATL   PNTR   WHSE   TRPL

Remarks/Instructions: _____

_____

_____

_____

_____

Shop Supervisor: _____ Date: _____ Work Order # _____

Work Order Status

Crew Assigned: _____ Date Scheduled: _____

Summary of Work Done: _____ Date Completed: _____

_____

_____

_____

_____

_____

Shop Supervisor: _____

Work Order Close Out

208

Physical Plant Use Only		Work Order Number

Part 1 - REQUEST (COMPLETED BY REQUESTOR)

TO: Physical Plant, Planning & Scheduling		Dept. Request No.

From: Name _____   Account No. _____

      Title _____   Location of Work:

      Phone _____   Building _____ Room _____

      Dept. _____ College _____   Other _____

Request for: _____ Estimate _____ Change Order   Special Requirements _____

      _____ Performance _____ Other   _____

Description of Work: _____

_____

_____

_____

Name of Contact _____   Phone _____

Requestor's Signature _____   Campus Address _____

(must have signature authority)   Date _____   Attachments _____

PART II - ESTIMATE (COMPLETED BY PHYSICAL PLANT)

TO:

Estimate   Remarks _____

      Labor _____   _____

      Material _____   _____

      Contract _____   Enclosures _____

      Contingency _____   Signature _____

      Total _____   Date _____

PART III - AUTHORIZATION (COMPLETED BY REQUESTOR)

To: Physical Plant Planning & Construction

Authorization to proceed _____

      Signature _____   Date _____

(Physical Plant Use Only)	A&E _____	Date _____
Disposition: 1. Work Order Assigned To: _____	Utilities _____	Date _____
2. Cancelled. Date _____	Maintenance _____	Date _____
3. Closed. Date _____	Other _____	Date _____

209

Plant Planning and Maintenance
Work Order Request Form

Date:	
Request Number:	
From (Department/School)	
Requested by Name:	
Phone Number/Ext.:	
Email Address:	
Location of work in school:	
Date Needed by:	
Contact Person:	
Contact Phone Number/Ext.:	
Description of work needed. If this is a capitol improvement, please give reason for need.	
Name of principal or administrator:	
Title:	

Save Name, Phone and School information as a cookie for future use? Yes ▾

Click here to submit your request.

About the Authors

GLEN I. EARTHMAN has spent 40 years in the field of education serving as a teacher, principal, Executive Director for school facility planning in the Philadelphia Public Schools, and finally as Professor of Educational Administration at Virginia Polytechnic Institute and State University in Blacksburg, Virginia. Dr. Earthman has served as a consultant to over 70 school systems across the country and overseas helping them with various school facility problems. He currently has Emeritus Faculty status at Virginia Tech where he continues to teach graduate courses on school planning and advises doctoral students in dissertation work. He served as the first Director of the ERIC affiliated National Clearinghouse for Educational Facilities in 1997–98. He has written extensively in the area of school facility planning authoring four textbooks and over 60 articles in periodical publications. His continuing research interests extend to all phases of school facilities, but he has concentrated on exploring the relationship between school building condition and student achievement.

LINDA K. LEMASTERS was a classroom teacher for 14 years before going into school administration, where she served as an instructional supervisor, director of human resources, and for 10 years as assistant superintendent supervising human resources; student services; budget and finance; food service; transportation; maintenance and engineering; and custodial, buildings, and grounds. She currently is an assistant professor of education administration and leadership in the Graduate School of Education and Human Development with The George Washington University, where she teachers graduate level coursework, advises students, and directs student research. Her areas of expertise include strategic planning, facilities management, and educational reform issues. She is conducting research concerning the effects of the facility on the learner and serves as president of Virginia Educational Facility Planners. Dr. Lemasters has many years of experience in building school facilities, working with outside contractors, interacting with school boards and governing bodies, and supervising support services employees.